The Author

W. O. S. SUTHERLAND, JR., is Professor of English at The University of Texas. He has taught previously at The University of North Carolina and Northwestern University. With Powell Stewart, he developed a method for indexing eighteenth-century periodicals which was demonstrated in the pilot volume *An Index of British Newspapers and Periodicals 1700*. He is the author of several articles on eighteenth-century periodicals and is the editor of *Six Contemporary Novels*.

The Art of The Satirist

ESSAYS

ON THE SATIRE OF

AUGUSTAN ENGLAND

by

W. O. S. Sutherland, Jr.

THE UNIVERSITY OF TEXAS

Contents

PREFACE
5

THE ANATOMY OF THE ART
9

OBJECT TO SYMBOL
THE RAPE OF THE LOCKE AND THE RAPE OF THE LOCK
ABSALOM AND ACHITOPHEL
HUDIBRAS *and the Nature of Man*
ARBUTHNOT'S *Simple Plan*
25

SATIRIC AMBIGUITY
THE VICAR OF WAKEFIELD *and the Kindly Satirist*
The Plot of RASSELAS
83

SATIRE AND THE USE OF HISTORY
Gulliver's Third Voyage
107

EPILOGUE
127

Illustrations and Typography by CYRIL SATORSKY

© 1965 THE UNIVERSITY OF TEXAS

Published by HUMANITIES RESEARCH CENTER, UNIVERSITY OF TEXAS

Distributed by the UNIVERSITY OF TEXAS PRESS, AUSTIN, TEXAS 78712

Library of Congress Catalog Card Number 65–64858

PRINTED IN USA BY THE UNIVERSITY OF TEXAS PRINTING DIVISION

Preface

The century of satire begun so notably in 1663 with the first part of *Hudibras* contains most of the great satires of English literature, but between the octosyllabic couplets of *Hudibras* and the Vicar of Wakefield's sermon on the Equal Dealings of Providence Demonstrated lies a range of artistry that defies a simple label. This book attempts to explore that range.

The first essay, The Anatomy of The Art, is devoted to the principles and assumptions distinctive of satiric writing. Each of the remaining essays is introductory to one of the great satires of the period, though at the same time the point of view from which it is written relates it to one of the larger critical heads of Object to Symbol, Satiric Ambiguity, or Satire and the Use of History. The underlying assumption in each essay is that satire should be read as art rather than propaganda, the assumption of most successful satiric criticism in recent years.

Although no attempt has been made to apply a mechanical plan of analysis, the subjects of the essays have been selected to assure that most of the vexing problems of satiric criticism are eventually met.

I wish to express my thanks to my colleagues Professors Leo Hughes and Robert L. Montgomery, Jr., for helpful suggestions. My thanks go also to Chancellor Harry H. Ransom of The University of Texas for his support. Finally, I acknowledge my long-standing debt to Professor Richmond P. Bond.

The Anatomy of the Art

NO ONE HAS MUCH TROUBLE IN POINTING OUT SATIRE, BUT AN attempt to describe or define it often arouses an uncomfortable feeling of inadequacy. Traditionally it is one of the genres, and formal verse satire supports the tradition. But a definition of formal verse satire can hardly do justice to works like *The Beggar's Opera* and *The Spectator*. As examples multiply, it becomes clear that satire can dominate an entire work or appear as a single paragraph in a four-volume novel. This trait has encouraged some critics to regard satire as an element or quality rather than a form itself. But if satire is a part of something else, a necessary part of the critic's task is to describe that "something else."

The difficulty competent critics often have in saying what satire is suggests that the fault may lie in the form of the question rather than in the critic's ability to answer. The question "What is satire?" apparently encourages answers made in terms of the purpose of the satiric author or in terms of the actual subject matter of the work of art. Unfortunately neither quality is distinctive of satire. If judged by purpose and subject matter, *Pilgrim's Progress* and *Gulliver's Travels* are members of the same class. Satire's traditional purpose is reform, a purpose that the literary artist shares with every parson writing a sermon. The satirist's traditional subject matter, vice and folly, is not very helpful either, for to speak with precision these words do not indicate a subject but an attitude on the part of the speaker. The Whig's patriotic action may be the Tory's treason. The king's mistress is, quite often, somebody's mother. It can be said that vice and folly do represent a continuity of attitude among satirists, for there is a unanimity of disapproval apparent in satire. By itself, however, this trait is not distinctive. *Pilgrim's Progress* again furnishes a useful touchstone.

Satire has been described and discussed perceptively by many critics.[1] A definition based upon the traditional and obviously inadequate concept of genre can still provide fruitful insights. Descriptions which themselves invoke the satiric spirit may be stimulating and illuminating even though they select characteristic rather than distinctive traits.

The chief point not fully developed by most critics is whether there is anything distinctive about the way the satiric author presents his material. What are the possibilities for literary presentation, and what is the relationship of satire to them? These two questions are of crucial importance for two reasons: first, for showing how satire works, and second, for demonstrating and stating explicitly that satire is fundamentally related to other literary techniques and that it has the same general purpose seen in other kinds of literature. Its assumptions are essentially aesthetic and only incidentally propagandistic. In order to be read with understanding, it must be read the same way other literature is. A general recognition of the fundamentally aesthetic nature of satire is a first step in releasing it from the bondage of its origins and milieu.

The paragraph that follows is not offered as any definitive theory, nor as the only way of classifying literary technique. It does have the virtue of showing simply and briefly the relationship of satire to other modes of presentation.

Literature is concerned with two different kinds of materials: presentation of conditions (description or activity) and statements of value. The literary artist uses each of these kinds in two different ways. He can present conditions by a dramatic method, in which the characters speak in their own persons, or by the narrative method, in which he stands in some way between the action and the audience. Neither the dramatic nor the narrative has inherent value, though it is usually given some sort by the author. In stating values, the author also has alternatives. The lyric mode, using the term *lyric* very broadly, is a statement of values which the author or a character or the persona accepts, one which the audience regards as credible. Contrasting values may be used, but it is characteristic of the lyric mode that it presents positively values which are acceptable. The ironic mode offers values which the audience sooner or later regards as unacceptable. The character or persona may not himself be aware that his values are not valid, or he may learn as the work develops. The audience, however, must know. Satire occupies a significant part of the ironic mode.

Satire, though a part of irony, is marked by three distinctive characteristics. First is a contrast in values. The author creates one set of values to act as a criterion; the other is the subject of the satire. The degree to which the criterion is obvious varies sharply from work to work; often it exists only by implication. But it must be present. Without a criterion an author must be either objective or sympathetic. A work like Rochester's *A Satyr Against Mankind*, since it holds no hope for improvement, does not expect man to

10

be rational. Yet, it still judges him against this impossible ideal. The naturalistic author offers a useful contrast to the satirist. The naturalist may see many of the same qualities which the satirist sees, may often present human life as a parallel to animal life. But the naturalist does not necessarily add a preconceived moral criterion. Lacking a criterion he cannot judge. He may show sympathy, but he shows it as a normal human response to some condition like pain. The satirist sees a moral discrepancy and shows disapproval. A master satirist like Dryden can show sympathy as he condemns. Goldsmith, Addison, Fielding, and Sterne can satirize yet remain sympathetic.

The values attacked by the satirist are usually stated in terms of "objects," and much of the scholarly energy expended on satire has been an exposition of the historical nature of these objects. Patently the level of propaganda was significant for the poet and his contemporaries, but with passing time this level becomes less and less important. In themselves political squabbles of the past are ephemeral. But great imaginative expression is not, for one of the qualities of its greatness is that it can transform a local situation into something meaningful to the generations that follow.

The second characteristic of the satiric mode grows out of the first. The poet indicates an unfavorable attitude toward the values which are the subject of the satire and a favorable attitude toward the values which act as the criterion. It is hard to separate statement and judgment, for the poet's attitude is almost always a part of his conception of the values. The satiric author may recommend virtue, but his chief end is to denigrate the values he is attacking. Sometimes he achieves this by his selection of material, more often by a special sort of exaggeration.

In order to denigrate his object, the satirist concerns himself with falsehood rather than truth, a concern that distinguishes the satiric presentation. The truth of a lyric, for example, may be fragmentary. As in the case of Yeats, it may not be scientific truth, but a truth sufficient and convincing within the poem. One of the great functions of metaphor is to arrive at some sort of truth. In his function as denigrator, however, the satirist is fundamentally opposed to the lyricist. In drawing Atticus in the *Epistle to Dr. Arbuthnot,* Pope is not trying to be true to Addison's character; rather he succeeds only if what he writes is untrue. The various authors attacked in the *Dunciad* were angry at being, as they thought, treated unfairly. Their anger was not only understandable, but justified. Pope did not tell the truth about them.

But the satirist's concern with falsehood is not haphazard, and he is not unconcerned with truth. Actually truth is as important to him as to any other writer, though in a different way, for the flower of falsehood must grow from a seed of truth. The character of Atticus is a misrepresentation if applied to Addison. Literally it is unfair to him. The characteristic upon which Pope built was, however, a true one or—just as good—widely accepted as true. Dryden's character of Zimri in *Absalom and Achitophel* may contain a larger grain of truth than the character of Atticus, but it remains as far as its object is concerned a misrepresentation. This paradox of literal truth as the basis of poet's falsehood is a *sine qua non* of satire.

The seed or seeds of truth are necessary for the poet's misrepresentation to be convincing, or at least appealing. It does not matter whether the seed is literally true or not so long as readers accept it or can be persuaded to accept it as true. It does, however, matter whether the seed of truth taken by the artist is relevant to his purpose. Dryden's Achitophel and the historical Shaftesbury are strikingly different. They overlap only slightly. They overlap, however, at significant places, and it is this significance that makes Achitophel relevant to Shaftesbury. Here the satirist walks a narrow line.

Relevance, then, qualifies the sort of truth which the satirist may use. Relevance also has a part to play in persuading the reader that the misrepresentation may be true. Dryden's *Mac Flecknoe* and Shadwell's *The Tory Poets* illustrate the point neatly. There is, or might be, a grain of truth in Dryden's characterization of Shadwell —under the name Mac Flecknoe—as dull. That dullness, further, is relevant to Dryden's poem, for dullness is a part of his theme. It is also relevant to Shadwell's character. In *The Tory Poets* Shadwell sought to defend Shaftesbury from Dryden's attacks in *Absalom and Achitophel* and to attack Dryden. One of the points of attack is the reputation of Dryden's wife. This passage is pure denigration which some of Shadwell's readers might be persuaded to accept, but whether acceptable or not as fact, it is essentially irrelevant to Shadwell's purpose.

The third and last characteristic of the satiric mode is that the reader is not really deceived, though he must never reveal that he is not. Reader and poet tacitly agree that the misrepresentation is not factual. The *Beggar's Opera*, for example, is not an accurate, literal representation of society. The audience recognizes this fact.

12

The author, though he nowhere acknowledges it, cannot expect the audience to think otherwise. There must, then, be an element of irony in the author's presentation. Failure to recognize this element means failure of the satire. William H. Whyte, Jr. tells of the business man who was tempted on a formal occasion to deliver a parody on after-dinner speeches. Fortunately, he did not, for he recognized that if some of his friends were not acute enough to understand that the speech was a misrepresentation they would resent him as well as the speech. In *The Shortest Way with Dissenters* Defoe posed successfully as a high-flying Tory who called for the blood of the Dissenters, all of which frightened his friends and chagrined his enemies. Defoe in the pillory is a strong reminder that the reader must not be misled.

Failure to understand this tacit agreement between author and reader is one of the pitfalls in using satire as a historical document. W. D. Christie in his *Life of Shaftesbury* has protested against the lack of truth and justice in Dryden's character of Shaftesbury in *The Medal*. But, of course, this protest has no relevance when made against a satire. Both the author and his perceptive reader realize that "historical accuracy" is not a meaningful phrase applied to a satiric portrait.

It is the absence of this ironic element which makes *Pilgrim's Progress* something very different from satire, though an analysis of Bunyan's purpose and subject matter reveal a deep kinship to those of the satirist. Vanity Fair has all the possibilities for a great satiric scene except ironic acceptance. The author believes in his scene and so does his audience. This element of belief places *Pilgrim's Progress* in the lyric rather than the satiric mode. *Sinners in the Hands of an Angry God* was a terrifying emotional experience because both Edwards and his congregation gave it credit. Yet today it does not seem so far from satire as the horrified screams of the Puritan congregation would suggest.

It would be wrong to conclude that there is always absolute understanding between author and reader. Some of Goldsmith's attitudes in the *Vicar of Wakefield* will always be a matter of debate. The ending of the book, for example, has been a subject for speculation. Whether certain speeches are overdone is a question for discussion rather than decision. But this ambiguity, far from being a blemish, is actually one of the reasons the book continues to attract. Sir Roger de Coverley, Parson Adams, and My Uncle Toby are other characters who succeed largely through ambiguity.

13

˖ This ironic element in satire, the agreement between author and reader, is not incidental or spontaneous, but a part of the creation. It may, indeed, be one reason some readers reject satire. The satiric creation does involve the emotions, but the reader cannot surrender them to the artist. If he does, he will feel, as W. D. Christie did, that the artist is betraying him. The satiric mode requires him to discriminate. For many readers, this demand is an interference with their emotional reaction. They are not willing, perhaps not able, to react with restraint. To them the ultimate emotion is not worth the expense of spirit. In addition, a part of the satiric creation is—to use the word loosely—grotesque, and many readers take no pleasure in its contemplation.

The diversity of the tone of satire grows out of the way authors vary the three elements that constitute the satiric mode. The author may weaken or strengthen the discrepancy between the criterion and the satirized object, or he may give more or less emphasis to the criterion. He may misrepresent very strongly or he may remain very close to his seed of truth. The extent of the misrepresentation is, of course, joined to the attitude which the author indicates. Finally, he may weaken the ironic agreement with his reader by creating something close to a serious, accurate statement of the case. Sir Roger de Coverley shows sympathetic handling of the gap between the criterion and the object. His virtues overbalance his faults, and his faults are often presented as rather harmless eccentricities. The tone of the *Spectator* papers should be contrasted to a piece like Swift's *A Modest Proposal* in which everything is done to emphasize the difference between the attitude of the English toward the Irish and the attitude which decent humanitarian and Christian principles would persuade anyone to take. The author's use of the seed of truth varies with every work. At one extreme stands Garnett's ghost in John Oldham's *Satyrs upon the Jesuits*. Garnett, the reputed fomenter of the Gunpowder Plot, is a blood-thirsty fanatic who raves through a heightened, inflamed monologue. At the other extreme are the claims for the literal, accurate representation of living men made for Hudibras, for Sir Plume in *The Rape of the Lock*, and for Col. Sellers in Mark Twain's *The Gilded Age*. The weakened ironic agreement ending in the lyric can be seen in Johnson's portrait of Charles XII of Sweden in *The Vanity of Human Wishes*. His description reads almost like one of the tragedies from Chaucer's *Monk's Tale*. Pope's character of Sporus in the *Epistle to Dr. Arbuthnot* illustrates the author tacitly in league with his readers. Sir Roger represents the audience constantly aware of an ironic contrast.

No one of the three elements works alone. All cooperate to create the tone of the satire. It is probably true, however, that the degree of misrepresentation—except as it involves introduction of the comic mode—has less influence on tone than either the emphasis placed upon the discrepancy between the two sets of values or the degree to which the author seems to accept his own misrepresentation.

The repeated warnings of recent years that the satirist speaks as artist rather than in his own person have focused attention on the use of the persona or assumed personality through which the satire is revealed.[2] Sometimes the artist favors direct revelation, sometimes indirect. The ingenue character is the means for indirect revelation. The early Gulliver shows how the ingenue can reveal and at the same time be an object of satire himself. The character of the direct method is the sophisticate, though it would be more descriptive to call him the moral man. The ingenue calls for intensive irony. The sophisticated narrator almost always leads to open moral judgment and denunciation.

The use of a persona in the formal verse satire can be very simple. There may be only one persona, the speaker of the poem, in which case the kind must be determined—a simple task—and the speaking itself judged in terms of the characteristics which are found. Most English satires, however, are more complex. In *Gulliver's Travels,* for example, the narrator is a character seen in dramatic perspective. The changes he undergoes in the course of the book complicate the concept of him as the author's "voice." The use of another persona such as the King of Brobdingnag and the Houyhnhnm master make it clear that the relatively uncomplicated technique usually used by Pope is not universal and that the interplay among the characters is as important as the characters themselves.

Writers of the eighteenth century usually insisted upon the moral nature of satire. The concept of satire here argues that though morality may be essential within one work, it is not a distinctive characteristic. Indeed, satire is not only not moral in itself, but because of its concern with falsehood and its dependence upon the discrimination of the reader is probably subject to perversion more often than lyric, or non-satiric, writing. It can be made to serve religion, morality, and good politics. But it can also be made to serve the opposition. Satire as a mode is amoral. It serves the poet. Though the technique is constant, the poet's standards are not. Morality lies in attitude, not in fact. The Whig's hero is the Tory's rebel: John Dryden's villain was John Locke's friend. Literary technique is disinterested.

Another traditional comment about satire is that it laughs its readers out of their vices and follies. Here there are two cruxes, one at *laugh* and one at *vices and follies.* That laughter is often associated with satire and is directed at some object is an observation frequently made. Actually laughter is only one result of satire. It happens when the comic and satiric are brought together. But the laughter is directed not at the follies and vices, rather at the misrepresentation which the artist has created. Laughter is certainly an indication that the misrepresentation is a success, showing as it does that the reader is on the side of the poet rather than on the side of the satirized object. But to achieve a moral end, the reader must go on to make a contrast between the misrepresentation and the ideal, recognizing the desirability of his achieving the ideal. Such a reaction from a reader is neither necessary nor characteristic. It has no connection with the aesthetic of the work of art. Laughter is a common reaction to satire just as it is, under certain conditions, to non-satiric exaggeration. But it is only one reaction and not necessarily a cleaning agent for morality.

The second crux, *vices and follies,* brings up the notion so frequently advanced in the eighteenth century that vices and follies, not crimes, constitute the proper object of satire. In 1734, one lesser writer in Aaron Hill's *Prompter* expressed the sentiment in capital letters: WHEN FOLLIES HAVE BECOME TOO GREAT FOR LAUGHTER, THEY ARE NO LONGER TO BE LAUGHED AT. The distinction seemed valid, perhaps because most eighteenth-century authors were interested in personal or literary satire. Literary satire does not deal with punishable crimes, and personal satire does not usually attack people who are in jail. The principle worked only when it was not tested. Eighteenth-century writers had only to look back at their predecessors in the last half of the seventeenth century to see that such a rule was an expression of preference rather than principle. Dryden's great political satires, for example, deal with heinous crimes. *The Medal* is subtitled "A Satire Against Sedition" and *Absalom and Achitophel* deals explicitly with treason. The distinction between what can and cannot be satirized does not lie in the seriousness of the

16

object. The distinction lies in whether there are two sets of opposing values. Tied in closely with this distinction is the question of whether the object can be misrepresented. Murder, for example, is not a normal subject for satire. Western culture considers the act reprehensible except under unusual conditions. It is difficult to misrepresent because it is a deviation from accepted conduct which is grotesque in itself and does not need to be overstated, or perhaps cannot very well be overstated. Society's attitude toward murder is so unanimous that the average reader would not be likely to have patience with an author who set out to express an unfavorable attitude toward it. Robbery, mayhem, rape, and similar crimes elicit the same reaction from most readers. Repulsive crimes do occasionally appear in satire, of course. Voltaire's *Candide* is successful as is Fielding's *Jonathan Wild*. In the case of Fielding's book, the opposing values were made credible because Wild was a criminal whose sense of values turned out to be believable when applied to at least one man of high station.

The eighteenth-century theorists also contended that insanity, physical deformity, and similar matters over which a person had no control were not fit objects for satire. Such a belief came from their concept of the moral purpose, not from the satire itself. Dryden made magnificent use of Shadwell's size in *Mac Flecknoe,* and the physical traits of Pope and Johnson were the constant objects of satires which were often successful, though not great. Physical deformity, especially when used symbolically, was obviously very effective, though its use can hardly be defended on humanitarian grounds.

The constantly reiterated statement that the purpose of satire is reform is one of the great unexamined shibboleths of English literature. Almost all writers have maintained correction, reproof, or reform as a legitimate end of their work. Is it an illusion, a conventional statement, or a valid purpose that can be achieved?

Though most writers claim reform as their purpose, evidence of their accomplishment is notably slight. John Gay in *The Present State of Wit* testifies to the spectacular success of the *Spectator* in reforming mores, though for comments of this sort most historians would prefer a solemn, humorless ass to the genius of Augustan wit. But complaints imply that satires were no more regarded than sermons. In *A Tale of a Tub* Swift remarks that "satire, being levelled at all, is never resented for an offence by any, since every individual person makes bold to understand it of others." Gulliver's letter to his cousin Sympson contains the striking cry, "I wrote for their amendment, and not their approbation." There is little evidence either way. Though it would be false to say satire has had no moral influence, it is certainly accurate to say it has not effected the reform for which it was ostensibly written.

It is easy to see why the satirist's influence upon his enemies has been slight.[3] Though critics may speak of satire as persuasive, this term is not descriptive of much of the best satire. Each satire has to be examined individually to see how it is written and for whom, but certainly no one expects *Hudibras* to "reform" any Presbyterians. The most cursory glance at the poem shows no such calculation on the part of the author. *A Tale of a Tub* with its talk of the universal pickle, Lord Peter's bulls, belching, and the rest could hardly expect to do less than offend sensitive Catholics and Presbyterians. And Pope, though he had proof positive that he was not changing the ways of his "dunces," rewrote and expanded his original version of the *Dunciad*, adding more and different dunces to "reform." Doubtless all these men hoped earnestly that the objects of their satire would mend their ways, but these works obviously are not expected to effect that change. It seems fair to conclude, actually, that those satirized would be offended and thereby confirmed in their course of action rather than swayed.

The one thing these works have in common, no matter what their authors hope for, is to state magnificently in imaginative form the values which their authors hold. They are written, if they are written for anyone besides the author, for people who hold the author's values. Many satires are stated in a form that could be persuasive. The *Epistle to Dr. Arbuthnot* has been analyzed in this way.[4] But even this poem would be written at most for the uncommitted rather than for Bufo and Atticus. The persuasive form seems to be merely conventional. This is not an uncommon situation. Many political speeches delivered to an audience made up of one party only take a persuasive form. They analyze both sides and come to a conclusion. But the persuasion is conventional, the conclusion anticipated with pleasure. Actually the speech, and in this case the satire, is primarily a statement of the values held by the speaker. Listeners accept what they already believe. It is a truism that sermons against the wicked are delivered only to the faithful. They are delivered and accepted not for their effect upon the wicked, but for their effect upon the faithful. *A Tale of a Tub* is a great and moving statement against evil values and in favor of traditional ideal values as Swift understood them. Men write from an urge to present deeply held values imaginatively, and satire can be read with understanding only if this underlying, though perhaps unstated, purpose is recognized.

The discussion of satire so far has been primarily concerned with "objects," and that is the place to begin since the author's technique is directly concerned with them. But objects of satire are notably short lived; they soon become faded and forgotten. The sad case of Sir Samuel Luke and the scholars is an instructive one. Everyone who has read an article on *Hudibras* knows that generations of scholars have regarded Sir Samuel Luke as the model of Sir Hudibras and one object of Butler's satire. Since the publication of Ricardo Quintana's "The Butler-Oxenden Correspondence,"[5] many scholars are no longer of that opinion. Sir Henry Rosewell becomes a leading candidate. But this change has had no effect on interpretations of the poem. If some enterprising scholar in the year 1984 went through all discussions of *Hudibras* and substituted Sir Henry Rosewell's name for Sir Samuel Luke's, one would hardly know the difference. There must be an object lesson here for the critic.

The identification by moderns of tangible objects of the satire can lead to serious distortion of the work of art and the poet's purpose, for the modern reader should not think of Shaftesbury, Hervey, or the rest as the simple target of the poet's disapproval. The poet may think that way, but the modern reader should not. The man Shaftesbury is immaterial. It is the values symbolized by the man that constitute the poet's object. The modern tends to think of Shaftesbury as a historical fact. History preserves the tangible, and what the great man did or said is important for itself and for what it led to. Dryden and his contemporaries lacked this dispassionate view of the man and his actions. They judged him by what he believed, by the values he held. Shaftesbury the man would not be important to Dryden, but what he had done and what he might do to confuse an already clouded future were overwhelmingly important. Dryden judges him by the values he holds, for this is the only way to predict his future actions. For Dryden, then, Shaftesbury is a symbol representing a complex of values rather than a human being with personal trials and triumphs. Shaftesbury the man is not Dryden's concern. Especially in personal, political, or literary satire it is accurate to say that the "object" of satire is actually a symbol. The author is at bottom attacking a set of inimical values.

Aside from a few literary curiosities, universal satire ought to be the concern of the critic. If it is to be read with understanding it will have to be read in terms of *values* rather than *objects*. Contemporaries of the satirist did not need to make this distinction. Modern readers do. Since the judgment of the satirist is dependent upon his own values, the modern reader should have a clear notion of the contrasting values of the work of art. Of course the way these values are understood and stated by the reader has a good deal to do with the significance he sees in the work of art. *Hudibras* is without question anti-Presbyterian. If the reader sees nothing more than this, the poem is hardly worth the time it takes for the modern reader to go through it. A clearer understanding of the contrasting values of *Hudibras* will let the poem speak powerfully to anyone who is concerned with man's view of himself and with his place in society and the universe.

There is a further compelling reason for detaching the satirist's symbol from the actual person or thing which is the "object" of the satire. Although the author begins with seeds of truth, as he builds he misrepresents. The greater the misrepresentation, the farther from the object, even as he sees it, he moves. If he builds logically from his seed he can retain credibility on the part of his contemporaries, though they and he know that he is building a misrepresentation. But his misrepresentation must be a logical expression of the values which the author is attacking. To the contemporary reader the satire is a paradox. It uses the object as a symbol and, normally, builds from a "true," relevant trait a picture that does not accurately portray the object. The modern reader does not have the advantage of a contemporary, for he lacks a predisposition toward the object which is to be used as symbol. He does, however, have an advantage the contemporary lacks. He does not associate with the symbol all the distracting values that must gather as his predisposition develops. Unfortunately much modern scholarship has succeeded in emphasizing the object at the expense of the universals. It is a platitude of literary histories that a great satirist confers undeserved immortality on his victims. In all fairness to the satirist, this is not true. It is the editors who have done so. The scholar, not the poet, has insisted that generations read Slingsby Bethel for Shimei or Sir George Browne for Sir Plume or the Duchess of Marlborough for Atossa.

It is a common statement among writers that satire flourishes in periods when men are agreed upon standards of conduct or belief.

Surely it is time this notion were categorically denied. England in the second half of the seventeenth century saw a great burst of satiric writing. Yet Englishmen were then divided in a way they have never been divided since. The early eighteenth century may seem a period of Augustan calm to later generations, but the merest acquaintance with lives of men of the period shows it to be a period of ferment, fear, and resentment. Actually satire is possible only when men do disagree. Periods of national unanimity, like the periods of war during the twentieth century, stifle satire rather than encourage it.

Satire is usually conservative politically and literarily because it answers the needs of those who are against change, but it is inadequate for those who want something different. A writer with a passion for reforming the world is usually concerned with the new rather than the old. His aesthetic work is in the non-satiric mode; his intellectual productions are credos, appeals, justifications, and statements of value. The conservative nature of satire is well illustrated in the seventeenth and eighteenth centuries by the literary attacks on the Royal Society and on Dissenters. Both represent new sets of values which men like Swift feared. But Swift's attacks cannot be characterized as merely conservative. He did not wish to preserve the actual values of Englishmen. These he detested. He was attempting to preserve the ideal values of his culture. These he defends, placing them in opposition to new as well as existing values. Men like Swift are conservatives in a rather special meaning of the term.

The satirist is not always politically conservative. In *The Shortest Way with Dissenters,* Defoe attacks those Englishmen who do not offer tolerance to Protestants outside the established church. A modern writer like Shaw in *Arms and the Man,* is trying to change long established views of his society. Such writers are still related to satirists who are more conservative culturally and politically, for they usually appeal to long established moral or cultural values even as they ask for change. Shaw appeals primarily to the ideal of the rational man, unfettered by tradition and dead values. Defoe appeals to the basic humanity of his readers to condemn those he attacks. Both writers depend upon ideal values of their culture.

Since the conservative almost always fights a losing battle, most satirists do not come to us in the role of precursors of our own beliefs. No matter how excellent the arguments of a monarchist may be, history has defeated them all. No matter how witty Fielding may be against the Royal Society, no one now takes him seriously. He was beaten before he started. Because they are so often on the losing side, satirists are seldom ranked as successful intellectuals. Instead, they are praised for being something rather second best, moralists. The nature of their battle and their weapon makes this unbalanced reputation almost inevitable. But it is often manifestly unfair. The kindest service the literary historian can offer the satirist is to place his work in such a context that the satirist's course will appear, if it can, as a genuine intellectual alternative as well as moral position.

Object to Symbol

THE RELATIONSHIP OF ART AND LIFE HAS ALWAYS BEEN THE
dominating problem of satiric criticism. Indeed, the propaganda of
a piece like *Hudibras* is so overwhelming that it continues to distract even after three hundred years.

The distraction is understandable, for it is encouraged by the
satiric authors themselves, partly by their frequent identification
of the speaker or narrator with the author and partly by their insistence that the satiric object is a specific person, institution, or
historical event. So much has been done with the mask or persona
in recent years that no one would now equate Swift and Gulliver or
Steele and Isaac Bickerstaff. But the flat statement that Atticus is
Addison or Achitophel is Shaftesbury still appears.

The historical exegesis of the satiric work may have been important to contemporary readers, but it is not a necessary part of
the aesthetics of the poem or narrative. To the author's contemporaries the object of attack and the symbol within the poem were
both vital and viable, but to the reader of the present, the historical
object, though it can be recreated, can never be animated. If a satire
still has appeal, the objects must symbolize something of wide or
universal significance. Like any other work of art, the satire must
transcend its origin. It follows, then, that the most important task
of the critic—here as elsewhere—is to deal with what is in the
poem rather than outside. History should be used, but as a means
to understand the work rather than as a source of aliases for the
characters who appear. The vocabulary of *Hudibras* presupposes
some knowledge of the Civil Wars in England, but it is a diminu
tion of the poem to interpret it in terms of Royalist and Puritan
merely.

The Rape of the Lock, Absalom and Achitophel, Hudibras, and
Epistle to Dr. Arbuthnot are in differing ways tied to history by
subject and purpose, but for the modern reader their historicity is
secondary. Their values and aesthetic are more important than their
origins or milieu. Each of the essays which follows takes this point
of view, though each approaches its subject in a way that seems
most appropriate to the work under discussion. "*The Rape of the
Locke* and *The Rape of the Lock*" attempts to show what Pope did
to turn a good satire into a great one. The essay on *Absalom and
Achitophel* is concerned with showing how the poem is an expres-

25

sion of values, not ignoring milieu but relegating historical fact to a non-essential role. *"Hudibras* and the Nature of Man" looks for evidence of universal application in a poem whose characters are usually confined to particular religious sects. Finally, *"Arbuthnot's* Simple Plan" shows how Pope's "characters" help create the poem, then discusses the significance of Atticus as Addison within the poem.

The Rape of the Locke and The Rape of the Lock

Although Arabella Fermor's name has been inscribed by many lesser mortals, it has never rivalled that of Belinda. *The Rape of the Lock* has always demanded an interpretation that transcended the quarrel which Lord Caryll was so anxious to settle.[1] Indeed, the variety of criticism written on Pope's mock epic is convincing evidence that Geoffrey Tillotson hardly exaggerates when he calls the poem "inexhaustible." But the poem was not always so. In 1712 was published *The Rape of the Locke. An Heroi-Comical Poem,* in two cantos. This was the poem which Addison characterized as *merum sal* and advised his friend Pope not to meddle with. But Pope, of course, did meddle, and in 1714 brought out *The Rape of the Lock. An Heroi-Comical Poem. In Five Canto's.* The speech of Clarissa was added in the 1717 version, and this, substantially, is the poem that is read today. The most common remark about Pope's revision is that in the later version he added the machinery—the sylphs. Tillotson identifies the additions as Belinda's dream, i 20–114; Belinda's toilet, i 121–148; the voyage up the Thames and Ariel's speech, ii 47–142; the game of ombre, iii 25–104; the sylph's attempt to divert the scissors, iii 135–146; Umbriel's visit to the cave of Spleen, iv 11–92; and a group of smaller changes toward the end of the poem all of which, except for the pedigree of the bodkin, concern the sylphs (iv 141 f.; iv 165 f.; v 53–56; v 83 f.; v 89–96; v 131 f.). Clarissa's speech is found in v 7–36. There were a few other very minor revisions.[2]

But the final result was not so much to expand as to transform the poem, for what began as a very fine poem ultimately became a work of genius. The revisions are the difference between excellence and greatness. An examination of the major changes which Pope effected will furnish an object lesson in the way a great satirist worked.

Pope's first important change was the addition of the speech Ariel makes to Belinda (i 20–114). Its most immediate effect is its influence upon the reader's concept of Belinda. To explain how the reader is affected it is necessary first to show how Belinda was described in the *Rape of the Locke.* Here are the lines that introduce her:

> *Sol* thro' white Curtains did his Beams display,
> And op'd those Eyes which brighter shine than they;
> *Shock* just had giv'n himself the rowzing Shake,

27

And Nymphs prepar'd their *Chocolate* to take;
Thrice the wrought Slipper knock'd against the Ground,
And striking Watches the tenth Hour resound.
Belinda rose, and 'midst attending Dames
Launch'd on the Bosom of the silver *Thames:*
A Train of well-drest Youths around her shone,
And ev'ry Eye was fix'd on her alone;
On her white Breast a sparkling *Cross* she wore,
Which *Jews* might kiss, and Infidels adore.
Her lively Looks a sprightly Mind disclose,
Quick as her Eyes, and as unfixt as those:
Favours to none, to all she Smiles extends;
Oft she rejects, but never once offends.
Bright as the Sun her Eyes the Gazers strike,
And, like the Sun, they shine on all alike.
Yet graceful Ease, and Sweetness void of Pride,
Might hide her Faults, if *Belles* had Faults to hide:
If to her share some Female Errors fall,
Look on her Face, and you'll forgive 'em all.
   This Nymph, to the Destruction of Mankind,
Nourish'd two Locks, which graceful hung behind
In equal Curls, and well conspir'd to deck
With shining Ringlets her smooth Iv'ry Neck. (i 13–38)

The presentation of Belinda is simple in that it is from the poet's point of view only. The "attending Dames" and "Train of well-drest Youths" show her pre-eminence, and mention of her "Favours" along with the sun imagery imply royalty. She is an attractive young lady whom the poet admires, but still views rather ironically. Though Love uses her locks, she is a human being toward whom the poet shows a fairly typical masculine attitude: he admires her, but he is not altogether serious. He is delicate, but clear. "Female Errors" and the ambiguity of "unfixt" mind make his point amply clear. This rather simple, single point of view makes a successful presentation, but she is uncomplicated either as a character or as a symbol. Nothing differentiates her from Phyllis, Amaryllis, or the legion of Floras.

   In the *Rape of the Lock* the addition of the dream introduces a new explicit point of view toward Belinda, that of the sylphs, particularly Ariel. The reader's first view no longer comes from a sympathetic, but mocking poet. It comes from her guardian sylph, whose first words disclose the significance of Belinda as well as his attitude toward her:

> Fairest of Mortals, thou distinguish'd Care
> Of thousand bright Inhabitants of Air! (i. 27–28)
>
> . . .
>
> Hear and believe! thy own Importance know (i.35)

Ariel's sense of values, which is the same as Belinda's, is introduced early and his values rather than the poet's dominate. Of course, the reader sides with the poet, but in the new version the poet's ethic is only one way of evaluating the action. Ariel's account of the origin of the sylphs makes clear a part of the significance of their scale of values.

> Think not, when Woman's transient Breath is fled,
> That all her Vanities at once are dead:
> Succeeding Vanities she still regards,
> And tho' she plays no more, o'erlooks the Cards.
> Her Joy in gilded Chariots, when alive,
> And Love of *Ombre,* after Death survive.
> For when the Fair in all their Pride expire,
> To their first Elements their Souls retire (i. 51–58).

The sylphs' values are the values of the society in which Belinda lives. It is proper, then, that they should dominate. To Ariel the coming action is a "dread event," just as it is to Belinda. The introduction of the sylphs brings to the poem a spokesman for these values.

But the sylphs introduce more than the values of society. They are religious creatures as well, though in the poem as in society religious and social values coincide.[3] The religious overtones of the sylphs indicate their seriousness within the cultural values of the *Rape of the Lock,* as well as the depth of Belinda's attachment to them. The religious symbolism is not completed until the scene of the toilet (i 121–148) is added. This scene discloses another attitude toward Belinda—how she looks at herself. Belinda is the priestess at the sacred rites of pride. It is not accurate to say that Belinda is priestess and goddess, for it is not exactly herself that she worships.

> First, rob'd in White, the Nymph intent adores
> With Head uncover'd the *Cosmetic* Pow'rs.
> A heav'nly Image in the Glass appears,
> To that she bends, to that her Eyes she rears (i. 123–126).

29

This is Narcissistic, but it is the "heav'nly Image" which Belinda worships. This image is an idealized projection rather than Belinda herself. The scene divulges Belinda's own attitude toward herself. The Image is more than a cultural value; it is something in which to believe and upon whose supernatural power she depends. Her two locks are symbols of her magical power.

The *Rape of the Lock* introduces in the first canto three explicit attitudes toward Belinda. The sylphs regard her as the fairest of mortals and of great importance. Belinda sees herself not only as representing the cultural values which she holds, but also as reflecting a special kind of power. The poet regards her partly seriously, partly ironically. He sees her as a woman, but an attractive one. Throughout the poem, however, he disguises his point of view by ironic agreement with Belinda's own evaluation.

These three attitudes toward Belinda grow out of two scales of value—those of the society of the poem and those of the poet. The values of Belinda's society are consistent. But the poet's point of view, and it is the one we are asked to assume, is ambivalent toward Belinda and her society. He disagrees, yet he sometimes seems to agree. The effect of the *Rape of the Lock,* much more than the *Rape of the Locke,* depends upon a recognition of conflicting values. An example is the line describing Belinda's toilet, "Puffs, Powders, Patches, Bibles, Billet-doux." The usual comment on this line is that it shows Belinda's confused values. But Belinda is not confused. This line illustrates accurately a sense of value which is quite clear to her. The line amuses the reader because he assumes a different set of values. Clarissa's statement will be discussed later, but even there Belinda's point of view is given some recognition.

The changes in Canto I have a marked effect on parts of the poem which are not themselves revised, but moved verbatim from one version to the next. For example,

> On her white Breast a sparkling *Cross* she wore,
> Which *Jews* might kiss, and Infidels adore.

is a tribute to Belinda's beauty, and an indication of her values. The ambiguity of the antecedent for *which* is amusing. In its new setting, the line takes on more meaning, for the ambiguity of the antecedent now represents a real ambiguity in Belinda's religion. The new use of religion in the poem also has an effect upon the reading of the line, "As Thou, sad Virgin! for thy ravish'd Hair." (ii. 10 *Locke*) In the *Rape of the Lock* she is more than a mere woman, for she is one of the "Virgins visited by Angel-Pow'rs," and the same line, now moved (to iv. 10 *Lock*) seems to give Belinda a place in a martyrology. The actual cutting of the lock also takes on a deeper significance, since Belinda has become more than a mere woman. Of course in the first version the locks had already been made symbols of Belinda's power and had been identified as the means by which Love bound her victims.

The game of ombre adds both wit and seriousness to the poem; at the same time it creates a highly significant change in structure. So many writers have expressed their delight in the game that it seems unnecessary to add further to this point. The game is literally apt, but it is also appropriate symbolically. It represents a normal pursuit of the nymphs and heroes of the poem, a pursuit which they took seriously yet one that is meaningless in itself. It is also useful for revealing the rather formalized nature of their conduct.

Just as important as its "delight," however, is the fact that it presents explicitly the relation between the Baron and Belinda. This relationship could be inferred in the *Rape of the Locke,* but as an inference it could not receive its proper emphasis nor make dramatic impact. The game is an allegorical presentation of their conventional relationship. The fact that it is conventional does not make it less serious or less real to the Baron or Belinda, though they may not consciously realize its full meaning. Pope sees the convention. But, as Cleanth Brooks says, "Pope knows too how artificial the social conventions really are and he is thoroughly cognizant of the economic and biological necessities which underlie them—which the conventions sometimes seem to mask and sometimes to adorn."[4] Mr. Brooks discusses with sensitivity the sexual material in the poem and its significance. Though the game of ombre is not the first introduction of sexual implications, it does show that this is the underlying, if not ostensible, relation between the Baron and Belinda.

Belinda is engaged in a conventional but serious "game" with the Baron. It is a game which she must win, for otherwise she loses her status and her charms. But she is caught in a paradox. Though defeat is fatal, complete victory is undesirable. She must eventually lose to the Baron—or to some man—but she must lose on her own terms. The Baron prefers her unconditional surrender. Belinda is playing a dangerous game. She knows that the initial advantage is with her, but whether she will eventually win or not is something she cannot confidently predict.

Belinda's selection of spades as trumps is recognition that her greatest strength and her greatest danger are really the same. The broad sabre of the hoary king of spades shares the sexual association of other swords and weapons, an association which the reader must be conscious of after reading lines 177–178 of Canto III. Her judgment is right, for the initial advantage is entirely with her. She is at first irresistible. The king of spades works for her, defeating the knave. But Belinda is not overwhelming, and after four tricks, spades begin to work for the Baron and against Belinda. The Baron is a dangerous opponent determined to win, and with Belinda's initial advantages spent, he begins to make progress. The Baron wants to win on his terms as his lavish use of diamonds indicates, especially his use of the "*King* who shows but half his Face." He does win her affections:

> The *Knave* of *Diamonds* tries his wily Arts,
> And wins (oh shameful Chance!) the *Queen* of *Hearts*.

But he does not win the "game" for Belinda recognizes her danger:

> At this, the Blood the Virgin's Cheek forsook,
> A livid Paleness spreads o'er all her Look;
> She sees, and trembles at th' approaching Ill,
> Just in the Jaws of Ruin, and *Codille*.

At the last moment she is saved by the king of hearts, who as a male would have second thoughts though his queen might act impulsively. Perhaps, even, he is the same as Love (ii, 23).

There is none of this "play" in the *Rape of the Locke*. The Baron, as far as Belinda was concerned, was the villain by chance. In that poem she does not distinguish him from her other admirers so he could not have received any encouragement. "Favours to none, to all she Smiles extends." Under these conditions the poet is right in contending the rape is a trivial thing.

The addition of the game of ombre brings with it a new relationship between the Baron and Belinda. This new relationship results in a new structure for the poem. Belinda is no longer the innocent victim of an admirer who is merely more adventurous than the others. She singles out the Baron and, for "Thirst of Fame," initiates the action. Her defeat of the Baron is his motivation for taking the lock. Since he cannot succeed by fraud, he will use force. Belinda's involvement means that the rape becomes a more serious matter. In addition, the Baron has won her affections, and the loss of the lock means the loss of her power over him. The card game, then, provides motivation, anticipation, and deeper meaning for the rape itself. It becomes the pivot upon which the action and meaning of the poem turn.

The addition of the Cave of Spleen makes no significant change in the development of the poem, but it does emphasize a shift in poetic technique which carries over from the *Rape of the Locke*. The first three cantos are mock epic. Belinda's values are ironically accepted and accorded the respectful poetic treatment which Homer, Virgil, Milton and other epic writers gave the values of their own poems. There is a good deal of fun here, but it all has an ostensibly serious purpose. Belinda's toilet is a religious ritual, and the card game is a meaningful struggle between Belinda and the Baron.

The fourth act,[5] the falling action, the descent underground is burlesque, a falling off in the poet's serious treatment of his material. No longer do we have the tension that a dual point of view—Belinda's and the poet's—makes possible. Though his touch remains light, it is the poet's ironic, masculine, amused point of view that dominates Canto IV.

> There *Affectation* with a sickly Mien
> Shows in her Cheek the Roses of Eighteen,
> Practis'd to Lisp, and hang the Head aside,
> Faints into Airs, and languishes with Pride;
> On the rich Quilt sinks with becoming Woe,
> Wrapt in a Gown, for Sickness, and for Show.
> The Fair-ones feel such Maladies as these,
> When each new Night-Dress gives a new Disease. (IV. 31–
> 38)

The theatrical machines, the teapots, pipkin, jar, goosepie, and bottles all demonstrate the technique of caricature rather than the mock epic. Thalestris' anger and Sir Plume's appearance and conversation all show the caricaturist's touch.

The technique of the fourth canto is consistent with that followed in most of the fifth, for the battle of the beaux and belles is also a burlesque action. Incidents like the toilet, the drinking of coffee, and the game of ombre were normal activities given value by Belinda and ironic value by the poet. But the battle of Hampton Court can take place only if the poet forces Belinda, the Baron, and their friends into unaccustomed roles, distorting them into caricatures of heroes and heoines. He need not—and does not—

make them ugly, but he must force them into battle.

Why does Pope shift his technique from mock epic to caricature? Why is he willing to build so carefully to the climax of the third canto, then shift to a burlesque Hades and a confused battle?

The shift in technique reflects accurately a change in attitude in Belinda. She lives in a society that has a carefully laid out code of behavior. As long as she follows that code, the poet treats her values seriously, though ironically. After the Baron cuts her lock, she foresakes her cosmopolitanism and acts in an unreasonable way, an action the poet can only explain as the effects of spleen. Now the charm of society gives way to the confusion of battle. The language remains serious, but the irony becomes more open in the genealogy of the bodkin, Jove's weighing the men's wits against the lady's hair, the charge of snuff, and the description of the lunar sphere. The poet's disapproval is clear.

In the light of the last two cantos, we can reread the opening lines of the poem.

> What dire Offence from am'rous Causes springs,
> What mighty Contests rise from trivial Things,
> I sing—

These lines describe the cutting of the lock in different and inconsistent ways: it is a dire offense and yet a trivial thing. Now we can explain these apparently contradictory lines. Through the third canto, as long as the poet took the values of Belinda's society seriously, the rape was a dire offense. But Belinda's society charms only so long as each member plays his part. Her anger and uncivilized resentment break the spell which she and her society hold over the poet. Judged against his own scale of values, the rape becomes a trivial thing.

Clarissa's speech of Canto V is the last addition which helps transform the poem.

> Say, why are Beauties prais'd and honour'd most,
> The wise Man's Passion, and the vain Man's Toast?
> Why deck'd with all that Land and Sea afford,
> Why Angels call'd, and Angel-like ador'd?
> Why round our Coaches crowd the white-glov'd Beaus,
> Why bows the Side-box from its inmost Rows?
> How vain are all these Glories, all our Pains,
> Unless good Sense preserve what Beauty gains:
> That Men may say, when we the Front-box grace,

Behold the first in Virtue, as in Face!
Oh! if to dance all Night, and dress all Day,
Charm'd the Small-pox, or chas'd old Age away;
Who would not scorn what Huswife's Cares produce,
Or who would learn one earthly Thing of Use?
To patch, nay ogle, might become a Saint,
Nor could it sure be such a Sin to paint.
But since, alas! frail Beauty must decay,
Curl'd or uncurl'd, since Locks will turn to grey,
Since painted, or not painted, all shall fade,
And she who scorns a Man, must die a Maid;
What then remains, but well our Pow'r to use,
And keep good Humour still whate'er we lose?
And trust me, Dear! good Humour can prevail,
When Airs, and Flights, and Screams, and Scolding fail.
Beauties in vain their pretty Eyes may roll;
Charms strike the Sight, but Merit wins the Soul.

William Warburton's edition of 1751 first carried the note that the
purpose of this speech was ". . . *to open more clearly the* MORAL
of the Poem . . . ." Many critics agree. Before Warburton's statement is accepted, however, the function of the lines should be
determined.

The speech is a contrast to that of Thalestris, Belinda's friend.
Thalestris had taken the loss seriously:

Gods! shall the Ravisher display your Hair,
While the Fops envy, and the Ladies stare!
Honour forbid! at whose unrival'd Shrine
Ease, Pleasure, Virtue, All, our Sex resign.
Methinks already I your Tears survey,
Already hear the horrid things they say,
Already see you a degraded Toast,
And all your Honour in a Whisper lost! (IV. 103–110)

These are Belinda's values, too, but neither Thalestris nor Belinda
sees that the social code which overlies the fundamental values of
society should not be taken as a good in itself. Such an error de-
stroys the charm and meaning of society. The shift to burlesque in
Canto IV was the poet's first indication; the burlesque battle is
another; and Clarissa's speech, the one sustained passage in the
poem not written from an ironic point of view, is the clearest. It is
placed appropriately both as a warning to Belinda and as a contrast

to the confusion that follows.

But before allowing Clarissa to condemn Belinda, the reader should understand what Belinda has lost and to whom she has lost it. She has, of course, two locks. But they are more than hairs.

> Love in these Labyrinths his Slaves detains,
> And mighty Hearts are held in slender Chains.

These locks have a magical power. Her strength is in her hair; and if it is cut she no longer has a supernatural superiority to men. She becomes a mere woman, and men are stronger than women. The Baron understands the virtue that lies in the locks, and the prize to which he aspires is more than the hair; it is power over Belinda. He prays for both the locks, though love grants him only half his prayer. He is, as far as Belinda is concerned, a sexual villain, though she would not have considered him that until he cut the lock. Until then he was only doing what any man would do, indeed what Belinda hoped and expected he would do. This game or battle by the rules was the way her society functioned. But the Baron's rape of the lock is an "unfair" attempt to deprive Belinda of her strength. But fair or unfair she has lost a part of her magical power over him, and may soon lose more. She tells the Baron:

> The Sister-Lock now sits uncouth, alone,
> And in its Fellow's Fate foresees its own;
> Uncurl'd it hangs, the fatal Sheers demands;
> And tempts once more thy sacrilegious Hands. (iv 171–174)

The Baron's conquest has been made possible by Love. Had Belinda been a coquette only, the sylphs could have protected her. But the "Earthly Lover lurking at her Heart," whom the game reveals to be the Baron, has made the loss of her power possible.

Belinda is, then, in great danger of losing the "game." Whether she will lose under favorable or unfavorable conditions she does not know. Thalestris thinks unfavorable. At this time Clarissa's speech makes the point that it is only a game and one whose real aim is lost if it is taken too seriously.

> How vain are all these Glories, all our Pains,
> Unless good Sense preserve what Beauty gains. (V. 16f.)

But Belinda refuses to recognize Clarissa's truth, and confusion follows. Sympathy for Clarissa must come from the poet alone, for she and he are the only ones who realize that Belinda can use her power best if she understands that it is a transient but powerful means of attaining deeper and more enduring values than those to be found at Hampton Court.

Clarissa is a realist who shares the poet's insight into society, but she does not share his view of love. The poet holds the common masculine view that love is amusing and really not very important; at least he tries to give the impression that he holds it. But the revised poem belies such an impression, for even as the poet asserts the triviality of the Baron's action, he proves its inexhaustible delight and significance.

Absalom and Achitophel

Absalom and Achitophel is one of the magnificent poems of the language, and even critics with reservations about its author's motives and historical accuracy have, through the years, joined in to praise it. But it has caused difficulty, partly because it is not easily classified and partly because it is tied so closely to historical events.[1] Anyone who calls it witty heroic must add that much of it is not heroic nor is it everywhere biting or witty. Often it is called a "party poem," though such a description requires the explanation that Absalom is treated tenderly and Achitophel is actually praised. If it is called an attack on the Earl of Shaftesbury, even the most superficial reader must wonder why it leaves its "main" subject so long. Dryden wrote the poem, so the usual story goes, at the request of Charles II. One can only regret that Charles was not more demanding if he could assist in such a remarkable production.

Absalom and Achitophel is often discussed in terms of a particular historical incident, but no one would argue that historical attitudes or events can be accepted as artistic justification. If the poem were tied ineluctably to history or grew inevitably out of royalist doctrine, one might spend his time as well on an inspired advertisement for Continental Can. Of course the poem did have an historic occasion, and it is an important dimension. But it is only one dimension. The poem itself is not fully revealed until its paradoxes and purpose are justified artistically. Nor is the greatness of its language explained until old labels are set aside and the poem itself examined.

Absalom and Achitophel is a narrative poem with the poet as the narrator who introduces characters and situations. The language of the poem depends directly upon the poet-narrator's assumptions about the material he has introduced. He constantly indicates his own attitude, ostensibly toward Biblical events. The fact that he exists after the time of the action is clear from the comment on the Plot:

> Succeeding times did equal folly call,
> Believing nothing, or believing all. (116–17)[2]

The intentional anachronism shows the same consciousness:

> Some thought they God's Annointed meant to Slay
> By Guns, invented since full many a day. (130–31)

Although his moral values can be worked out in detail for various situations, in general the poet believes in stable government, the rights of the king, integrity in men of high station, loyalty, gratitude, love and mercy. The poet is a moral man.

If the language of the poem is looked at as an attempt by the poet to express a situation and a value simultaneously, then there is no "language of the poem." There is only the language of the poet in a particular situation. The determining factor is not a decision to write heroic satire or even a witty heroic poem. The controlling factor is the poet's decision to express poetically his own attitude or values about a series of occurrences. Such a view of the poem explains such discrepancies as the witty treatment of the king in the early lines and the heroic treatment later. It accounts for the contemptuous treatment of Corah and the respectful treatment of Achitophel.

The opening lines, which explain Absalom's illegitimate birth, are concerned with sex. The poet's attitude is certainly not serious. He is witty, light, and in good punning form. The humorously allusive "When man, on many, multiply'd his kind," the surprisingly frank metaphor of Michal, "A Soyl ungratefull to the Tiller's care," and the acceptance of copulation as a religious duty have all the marks of informal, amusing narrative. The description of Absalom, which follows, is not so amused, more straightforward. He is both praised and blamed, though so is David.

> What faults he had (for whom from faults is free?)
> His Father could not, or he would not see.
> Some warm excesses, which the Law forbore,
> Were constru'd Youth that purg'd by boyling o'r:
> And *Amnon's* Murther, by a specious Name,
> Was call'd a Just Revenge for injur'd Fame. (35–40)

Dryden abandons the wit of the early lines of the poem because it is not in keeping with his point of view toward Absalom. He uses an innocent figure when he speaks of excess "purg'd by boyling o'r," but this figure seems less innocent as the poem develops and heat gathers more and more unfavorable connotations. It takes on overtones of danger when the poet uses a parallel figure a hundred lines later:

> This Plot, which fail'd for want of common Sense,
> Had yet a deep and dangerous Consequence:
> For, as when raging Fevers boyl the Blood,
> The standing Lake soon floats into a Flood;

And ev'ry hostile Humour, which before
Slept quiet in its Channels, bubbles o'r:
So, several Factions from this first Ferment
Work up to Foam, and threat the Government (134–141).

Dryden adopts a different tone and different imagery when he begins his description of the Jews. His wit is bitter and his imagery contemptuous.

Those very *Jewes,* who, at their very best,
Their Humour more than Loyalty expresst (61–62).

(Gods they had tri'd of every shape and size,
That God-smiths could produce, or Priests devise:) (49–50)

This is not heroic treatment. The heroic assumes an individual whose personal actions are of great consequence in the state. Further, he bears a personal moral responsibility for his actions. The Jews are treated as a group, and it is the assumption of the poet that groups are morally reprehensible and irresponsible. The description of the Jews makes clear that the fundamental cause of the threatened revolt against David was not the plot, nor Achitophel, but the desire for liberty in a people who had been treated too mildly.

These *Adam*-wits, too fortunately free,
Began to dream they wanted libertie. (51–52)

Achitophel is an opportunist who takes advantage of the evil nature of "God's pamper'd people."

But, when to Sin our byast Nature leans,
The carefull Devil is still at hand with means:
And providently Pimps for ill desires. (79–81)

Still acting opportunely, "The wish'd occasion of the Plot he takes." Achitophel can have hopes of success only if this bias to sin already exists. The allusion to the devil and the term "*Adam*-wits" creates a new symbol—the symbol of the tempted and the tempter. Significantly the first use of the symbol comes not with Absalom and Achitophel, but with the Jews and Achitophel. The parallels are clear. The Jews' desire for liberty parallels the concept of original sin. Achitophel, the Devil, persuades the Jews to defy David, God. The means Achitophel uses is guilty knowledge, the Plot.

This concept of the Jews explains the poet's attitude toward them. They cannot be heroic because they are not conceived of as individuals. Yet, they have a grievously sinful flaw for which they must be condemned. They are guilty—symbolically—of original sin. They are, therefore, treated with bitter contempt. Their original sin is the initial sin of the poem.

The introduction of Achitophel brings a new notion into the poem: the individual who controls his own actions, who persuades others, and who bears personal responsibility for his own actions. Further, what he does makes a difference to the state. The fact that he is evil does not keep him from being great. Although there is variety in the description of Achitophel, it is clear that the poet regards him as a great man and is using here language different from that used to describe, for example, the Jews. The paradox of the great, bad man who could have been a great, good man finds its outlet in the paradoxical language of this section. Almost any line serves as an example.

> A daring Pilot in extremity;
> Pleas'd with the Danger, when the Waves went high
> He sought the Storms; but, for a Calm unfit,
> Would Steer too nigh the Sands, to boast his Wit.
> Great Wits are sure to Madness near ally'd;
> And thin Partitions do their Bounds divide. (159–164).

As the poet reaches the point in his narrative at which action begins, he recognizes that narration is no longer adequate. He must present the direct speech of the characters themselves. The speech of the characters is heroic, though the heroic has been adumbrated in the description by the poet.

Achitophel and Absalom speak heroically because the poet conceives the heroic to be their nature. One is the son of the king; the other is the evil man trying to persuade him to treason. What happens has great repercussions in the state. These men are also of great significance because they show symbolically the devil tempting a man. In this temptation there is a personal responsibility on both sides. What happens is of great importance, for the struggle of the devil for a man's soul is the most meaningful of all struggles. This is not a very accurate parallel to *Paradise Lost*. The Jews' treason against David parallels the temptation of Adam and Eve. The temptation of Absalom is meaningful only against a background of the fallen Jews. It represents, actually, a much closer parallel to *Paradise Regained*.[3] Absalom is *a* son of God, but not the *true* Son of God, just as he is *a* son of David, though not the *true* (legitimate) son. As the Devil tells the Son of God:

41

> ... thou art called
> The Son of God, which bears no single sense;
> The son of God I also am, or was,
> And if I was, I am; relation stands;
> All men are sons of God (*PR*, IV, 516–20).

Absalom is a son of God, but a false messiah. The parallel to
Christ's temptation makes a meaningful symbol in the poem. Absalom's decision can, to some extent, help decide whether the
people will be directed toward salvation or damnation. It also, of
course, has individual significance for Absalom. As a parallel to
Paradise Lost the temptation has individual significance just as
every man's temptation parallels that of Eve and Adam, but it is
not the first or greatest sin. The Son of God's speech in Book III
of *Paradise Regained* is instructive in showing the measure of
Absalom's delusion. The true Messiah judges better:

> Thou neither dost persuade me to seek wealth
> For empire's sake, nor empire to effect
> For glory's sake, by all they argument.
> For what is glory but the blaze of fame,
> The people's praise, if always praise unmixed?
> And what the people but a herd confused,
> A miscellaneous rabble, who extol
> Things vulgar and, well weighed, scarce worth the praise?
> They praise, and they admire they know not what,
> And know not whom, but as one leads the other;
> And what delight to be by such extolled,
> To live upon their tongues and be their talk,
> Of whom to be dispraised were so small praise,
> His lot who dares be singularly good?
> The intelligent among them and the wise
> Are few, and glory scarce of few is raised.
>   (*PR*, III, 44–59)

The reader of *Absalom and Achitophel* realizes the extent of Absalom's delusion by Dryden's image of sexual seduction:

> Th' Ambitious Youth, too Covetous of Fame,
> Too full of angells Metal in his Frame;
> Unwarily was led from Vertues ways;
> Made Drunk with Honor, and Debauch'd with Praise.
> Half loath, and half consenting to the Ill. (309–313).

Achitophel and Absalom are conceived of by the poet as heroic figures and speak appropriately. But it is not enough to call their language heroic, for heroic language depends upon more than epical cliches, oratorical devices, and formal syntax. There must be heroic concepts and heroic assumptions behind the language.

> Auspicious Prince at whose Nativity
> Some Royal Planet rul'd the Southern sky;
> Thy longing Countries Darling and Desire;
> Their cloudy Pillar and their guardian Fire:
> Their second *Moses,* whose extended Wand
> Divides the Seas, and shews the promis'd Land:
> Whose dawning Day, in every distant age,
> Has exercis'd the Sacred Prophets rage:
> The Peoples Pray'r, the glad Deviners Theam,
> The Young-mens Vision, and the Old mens Dream!
> Thee, Saviour, Thee, the Nations Vows confess;
> And, never satisfi'd with seeing, bless. (230–241).

This is heroic, but the concept which is conveyed by image, symbol, allusion, and statement is a false one. Achitophel is using every means to persuade Absalom that he is the Messiah, but of course he is not. The same falseness is conveyed when Achitophel speaks of David's being called by Fortune, for David was called by God. The simile of David as the Prince of Angels "tumbling downward with diminish'd light" is another. Achitophel's speech is still poetry. It is still heroic poetry. But it is satanic in its values for it creates, essentially, a vision of falsehood rather than a vision of truth.

Absalom is a paradox, and his speech reflects it. As an illegitimate son he has high rank, but his royal blood is not recognized. The spirit which he has inherited from his god-like father urges him to greatness, but the condition of his mother restrains him. He has, therefore, reason to support the established order, but also reason to rebel against it. This paradox is reflected in his speech, which breaks clearly at line 363. The break is in more than subject matter. The early part of the speech is straightforward and in a reflective manner rather than in an emotional key. The sigh which he emits indicates the tenor of the speech. The second part of the speech is different. It expresses his ambition, and he shifts to exclamation and excited repetition. He begins to use imagery, and most of it appropriately refers in some way to rising and falling.

43

Achitophel's second speech, which convinces Absalom, ends with convincing arguments because its language in the final lines takes advantage of the paradox of Absalom's nature:

> He fears his Brother, though he loves his Son,
> For plighted Vows too late to be undone.
> If so, by Force he wishes to be gain'd,
> Like womens leachery, to seem Constrain'd:
> Doubt not; but when he most affects the Frown,
> Commit a pleasing Rape upon the Crown.
> Secure his Person to secure your Cause;
> They who possess the Prince, possess the Laws. (469–476)

Absalom is betrayed by qualities which, under different circumstances, would lead to greatness. But the paradox in his nature is a weakness and defeats him. His mind is not so great as he believes, for he is unable to see the truth about Achitophel. His speech with its incoherence and self-contradictions was a symptom of his inability to command men and fortune. David comments on this weakness:

> Poor pitied Youth, by my Paternal care,
> Rais'd up to all the Height his Frame coud bear:
> Had God ordain'd his fate for Empire born,
> He would have given his Soul another turn. (961–964)

The poet closes his comments on Absalom with elevated language, but as he moves on to Absalom's new friends, his language becomes more colloquial and his tone contemptuous. The section concerned with the Jews who "for interest sought t'embroil the State" has, appropriately, images dealing with business.

> These were for laying Honest *David* by,
> On Principles of pure good Husbandry. (507–508)

The Levites are associated by the poet with animals. They are called "deepest mouth'd," a "Pack," a "herd," and a "breed." Dryden gives ironic agreement to their smug self-satisfaction:

> Born to be sav'd, even in their own despight;
> Because they could not help believing right. (539–540)

The unheroic language which is typical of the narration as opposed to the action is again evident.

The characters of Zimri, Shimei, and Corah exemplify the in-

44

stability, narrow self-interest, and contemptible irrationality of the opposition to David. The appropriateness of the antitheses which develop the "character" of Zimri has been pointed out before and does not need to be quoted again. The same technique is used, though less profusely, in handling the "character" of Shimei. The first of his "character" demonstrates his misconception of the Christian religion, the attitude growing out of "Zeal to God, and Hatred to his King." The phrases "Cheat and Pray" and "pious Hate" are two brief examples, but the perversion of the phrase in St. Chrysostom's prayer is the wittiest and bitterest example:

> When two or three were gather'd to declaim
> Against the Monarch of *Jerusalem*,
> *Shimei* was always in the midst of them. (601–603)

The latter part of the "character" shows his religious reasons for miserliness. Where the instability of Zimri had been indicated by an antithesis within the line itself, the "character" of Shimei makes more use of the closed couplet with the situation in one line and a reason or developing statement in the other.

> His Cooks, with long disuse, their Trade forgot;
> Cool was his Kitchen, tho his Brains were hot.
> Such frugal Vertue Malice may accuse,
> But sure 'twas necessary to the *Jews*:
> For Towns once burnt, such Magistrates require
> As dare not tempt Gods Providence by fire. (620–625)

The ironic contemptuous treatment of Corah climaxes the attack on the friends of Absalom. Corah is a liar who is believed, and the poet's effort is directed toward making his language appropriate to this most notable quality. The ironic treatment accords with this end. Though the poet's detestation may easily be seen, ostensibly he has presented Corah favorably. Dryden's use of the couplet form contributes further to the ironic treatment, as he frequently makes the second line an ironic, anti-climactic contrast to the first:

> Yet, *Corah*, thou shalt from Oblivion pass;
> Erect thy self, thou Monumental Brass:
> High as the Serpent of thy metall made,
> While Nations stand secure beneath thy shade.
> What tho his Birth were base, yet Comets rise
> From Earthy Vapors ere they shine in Skies.
> Prodigious Actions may as well be done

By Weavers issue, as by Princes Son.
This Arch-Attestor for the Public Good,
By that one Deed Enobles all his Bloud.
Who ever ask'd the Witnesses high race,
Whose Oath with Martyrdom did Stephen grace? (632–643)

The same technique of ironic contrast is followed by Dryden in the ambiguous words, images and allusions selected for the passage. Beneath an apparent favorable meaning lies another sinister interpretation. The first line, for example, leaves unanswered the question of whether Corah will live in fame or infamy. In the second line, "Monumental Brass" is ostensibly a symbol of eternity, but beneath lies the meaning of monstrous effrontery and an even more sinister symbol of Corah as the sepulchral tablet for those against whom he testifies. The serpent was at one time a protection for the people of Israel against the bites of snakes; later it became an idol to which they sacrificed. Nor should the relation between serpent and Satan be forgotten here. In the line that follows, "shade" can mean protection or being cut off from the source of life, light, and glory. The use of "Comets," "Prodigious," and "Arch-Attestor" has the same effect of open approval masking sinister hidden meanings. The use of the martyrdom of Stephen is a little different from the others. The poet naïvely introduces it to prove an almost irrelevant point, but the sophisticated reader knows that the witnesses against Stephen were suborned and recognizes that their charge is very similar to that made by Corah: "For we have heard him say that this Jesus of Nazareth shall destroy this place, and shall change the customs which Moses delivered us." (Acts 6:14) One of the interesting points about many of these images and allusions is that though they seem to have some genuine relation to religious values, the sinister interpretation reveals this relationship to be specious. Using the pun *Prophet/profit*, this technique holds for a line like "But, where the witness fail'd, the Prophet Spoke." (655) "A church Vermilion, and a *Moses's* Face" provides an ironic explanation of Corah's appearance. But Dryden expects his readers to remember that the older translations gave Moses horns rather than a shining face. Corah with a red face and horns becomes an image of the devil. These ambiguous phrases and ambivalent symbols are, of course, witty. But they are much more than that. They are a brilliant adaptation of language to the poet's purpose.

After the description of Corah comes Absalom's speech to the people, followed by the poet's description of Absalom's progress and then by the poet's own comments. This latter section is interesting because it is emotional, but not heroic. These comments by the poet are almost wrung from him by events. First he describes Absalom treated as the Messiah, then the machinations of Achitophel. This leads him to cry out in disbelief:

O foolish *Israel*! never warn'd by Ill,
Still the same baite, and circumvented still!
Did ever men forsake their present ease,
In midst of health Imagine a desease;
Take pains Contingent mischiefs to foresee,
Make Heirs for monarcks, and for God decree?
What shall we think!

This section of the poem, lines 753–810, is structured about a series of rhetorical questions upon which the poet comments. The first questions are built around the proposition that the people have no right to make a king. The last question points out the imprudence of doing such a thing. This is not really reasoning in verse, for the questions are not so much intellectual inquiries as emotional affirmations. The comments have the same quality, as this symbol of a world of perverted values shows:

Then Kings are slaves to those whom they Command,
And Tenants to their People's pleasure stand. (775–776)

The use of emotional allusion prevents rational consideration:

All other Errors but disturb a State;
But Innovation is the Blow of Fate.
If ancient Fabricks nod, and threat to fall,
To Patch the Flaws, and Buttress up the Wall,
Thus far 'tis Duty: but here fix the Mark:
For all beyond it is to touch our Ark. (799–804)

This image is different from those used in the description of Corah. Although the religious nature of the allusion is not revealed until the last line, it is not a contrast but a sudden warning. It touches upon emotions of fear and apprehension of divine vengeance. Insofar as it is admonitory, it is formal, but it is not intended to "elevate" the emotions.

Dryden does actually identify an example of elevated language in *Absalom and Achitophel*, the description of Barzillai's son, lines 831–853. This section shows formal language, apostrophe, stately syntax:

> Thy force, Infus'd the fainting *Tyrians* prop'd:
> And Haughty *Pharoah* found his Fortune stop'd.
> Oh Ancient Honor, Oh Unconquer'd Hand,
> Whom Foes unpunish'd never coud withstand! (842–845)

But these mechanical manifestations are outward signs. The elevation grows from the effect of the material on the poet. Here, for example, is an apostrophe and an image: it concerns the death of Barzillai's son,

> Oh Narrow Circle, but of Pow'r Divine,
> Scanted in Space, but perfect in thy Line! (838–839)

The emotion of the exclamation is possible only because the poet has a subject capable of arousing emotion, but the depth of the emotion conveyed is achieved by the use of this particular image. The "perfect in thy Line" means the completion of the young man's own circle or line of life. It means the perfection of his life. It means perfection in his ancestral line. And his death means the end of his branch of the family line. Behind all this is the circle as the symbol of eternity. The mechanical qualities of the sublime are present only because they grow naturally out of the poet's attempt to express something about the young man who has died. The figure compresses several related concepts. The language is formal because of the persons addressed. The syntax is abrupt because the poet speaks with emotion. The sublime here, and in the rest of this brief part, grows out of the attempt of the poet to express his concept of his material.

The final speech of David also illustrates the heroic. David is an individual of great importance. What he does affects many men. He can choose his own course of action, and he recognizes the consequences of his choice. Finally, the poet presents him at a crucial point in his career and in the history of his nation. But rapt emotion is not characteristic of this speech, for it is inappropriate. David is making an intellectual decision. He debates it. In this debate he shows himself to be wise, patient, merciful, and just. These are qualities for which a low key is appropriate. He does begin one soaring figure of speech, but his mercy toward and love for his son interrupt:

Kings are the publick Pillars of the State,
Born to sustain and prop the Nation's weight:
If my Young *Samson* will pretend a Call
To shake the Column, let him share the Fall:
But Oh that yet he woud repent and live!
How easie 'tis for Parents to forgive! (953–958)

The close of David's speech, lines 1010–1025, is a prophecy made in the ringing language of formal rhetoric.

By their own arts, 'tis Righteously decreed,
Those dire Artificers of Death shall bleed.
Against themselves their Witnesses will Swear,
Till Viper-like their Mother Plot they tear:
And suck for Nutriment that bloody gore
Which was their Principle of Life before.
Their *Belial* with their *Belzebub* will fight;
Thus on my Foes, my Foes shall do me Right:
(1010–1017)

The words in the line following David's speech, "Th' Almighty, nodding, gave Consent," prove this to be not only a vision of the future but of divine justice as well. The vision is an emotional climax to the speech and a dramatic climax to the poem. It is also a symbolic climax, for it identifies the true Messiah.

Just as the description "heroic" fails to do justice to the language of *Absalom and Achitophel,* so also does the label "party poem."

The world of the poem is as complex as the world of John Dryden. In a mere party poem virtue and villainy are simple matters. In *Absalom and Achitophel* they are not. Achitophel, for example, is a circumscribed villain. His power of evil is opportunistic, not absolute. Dryden makes very clear that his evil is dependent upon the earlier sinful desire of the Jews for liberty. Achitophel is like the devil in that he is a fallen angel and the leader of the opposition to God's vicegerent. But Dryden is not a Manichean. The devil cannot create evil. Were it not that "man is very far gone from original righteousness, and is of his own nature inclined to evil," the devil and Achitophel would be helpless. Critics have remarked upon the way Dryden has emphasized Achitophel's earlier virtues and service to the state. But this earlier service enhances the similarity of Achitophel to the devil. Nor is it

49

an inconsistency, for Achitophel is not inherently evil. He was a virtuous man of great ability who sinned because of ambition. What was in moderation a virtue becomes in excess a sin, though it is a "godlike sin." This same excess led the young Absalom from the paths of virtue.

But the fall of Absalom has more complex causes. He is, it is true, placed in a situation not of his own making, and Achitophel tempts him by appealing to what would be one of his finer qualities, if it were kept in bounds. But David is also at fault for being too merciful, too loving toward his son. Mercy and love are godlike virtues, but David has been too indulgent. Nor is this indulgence limited to Absalom. He has acted in the same way toward his subjects. He recognizes this fault in his speech and cites specific points on which he will no longer yield:

> Votes shall no more Establish'd Pow'r controul,
> Such Votes as make a Part exceed the Whole:
> No groundless Clamours shall my Friends remove,
> Nor Crowds have power to Punish e're they Prove:
> For Gods and Godlike Kings their Care express,
> Still to Defend their Servants in distress. (993–998)

No moral man, according to Dryden's assumptions, could condone the action of Absalom, but to understand all is to forgive much.

The world of *Absalom and Achitophel* is not divided neatly into good and evil, right and wrong, or happy and unhappy. Even the most virtuous men come to grief. The paradox of excess of virtue in David is one illustration. The friends of Absalom show the undeserving prospering. The friends of David illustrate even more clearly the complexity of life. Jotham's piercing wit and pregnant thought did not prevent him from trying the "worse a while" before he "chose the better side." Of Amiel the poet asks "who can Amiel's praise refuse?" Yet Amiel is out of place. And Barzillai, whom the poet ranks first of David's friends, bears the greatest load of disappointment and grief in the death of his son. The expression of such values as these deserves to be called honest rather than polemical or one-sided.

Behind this poem is a wise tolerance of human nature, for in life there is much to be endured by all men. Righteousness is no breastplate, for the hearts of the most virtuous are most deeply touched. But sympathy does not prevent the poet from passing moral judgment. The sins toward which he shows the most respect are those which are most "godlike," ambition especially. The sins toward which he is most contemptuous are political apostacy (the Jews), narrow self-interest (Shimei), and hypocrisy (Corah). These are the assumptions of a tolerant, high-minded man, not those of a party poet.

The satiric technique is practiced on the crowd, their representatives, and Achitophel. There is at least a grain of truth in the presentation of each, but whole truth is nowhere seen. Among great satires there seems to be no relation between the degree of distortion of the actual objects and the excellence of the work. That is perhaps true because a great satire must be judged in terms of universals rather than in terms of one particular situation. And the theme of temptation and fall is conceived of by Dryden in universal terms. It occurs either implicitly or explicitly in the poem in the fall of Satan, the fall of Adam, the sin of the Jews, the sin of Achitophel, the sin of Absalom, the sin of the Earl of Shaftesbury, and the sin of the Duke of Monmouth. Along with these the reader is constantly aware of the rejection of Satan by the Son of Man. This is the sort of poem in which the universal is a part of the conscious concept of the artist.

Absalom and Achitophel is a mature poetic statement about sin, temptation, and the conditions of human life. It is also a statement about sons—the Son of God, the son of David, the son of Barzillai, the sons (subjects) of the king, and even the son of Achitophel. One of the greatest disservices which older historical scholarship has done to the poem is to persuade critics that the tribute to Barzillai's son was motivated by personal rather than artistic considerations. Dryden identifies it as a high emotional point of the poem. It has reason to be, for it introduces, delicately, a tribute to the faithful son. Barzillai's son has all the virtues of Absalom, but along with it he is dutiful. Against this background the lines

> Now, free from Earth, thy disencumbred Soul
> Mounts up, and leaves behind the Clouds and Starry Pole.
> (850–851)

show the fate of a virtuous soul, an end which Absalom cannot expect. Absalom's attempt to mount an earthly throne, and his submission to the tempter prevent him. Barzillai's son serves in the poem as an ideal and as a warning. The fact that this virtuous young exemplar is dead is another measure of Dryden's honesty.

There are many "languages" in *Absalom and Achitophel,* for the poet deals with many men and many ideas. But it is not enough to look at the language of particular sections, for each part of the poem—each word of the poem—occurs in a context, and the relationship thus created has, of course, its own effect on word, allusion, image, symbol. Chiefly by repetition, Dryden builds several conditions which significantly affect the language of the poem.

The most notable is the underlying motif of temptation, fall, betrayal, forgiveness, mercy, and justice. This religious imagery and symbolism can be looked upon as a technique of presentation. But it is a good deal more than that. Its use makes clear the poet's assumption that political order is a reflection of and tied to divine order. Political rebellion is a kind of religious rebellion. Rebellion against the king is rebellion against God. Those who would repudiate the principles upon which the state was founded would repudiate the principles upon which religion was founded.

> If those who gave the Scepter, coud not tye
> By their own deed their own Posterity,
> How then coud *Adam* bind his future Race?
> How coud his forfeit on mankind take place?
> Or how coud heavenly Justice damn us all,
> Who ne'er consented to our Father's fall? (769–774)

The language of this poem proclaims that there is no such thing as mere political treason. Treason to the king is rebellion to God. This assumption on the part of the poet invests the poem with high seriousness of purpose. The imagery of the poem grows not merely from need for a technique but from the basic assumptions and values of the poet.

The recurrent motif of son and father is a part of the religious imagery, but it has an independent use as well. It helps the poet to establish the conditions of human nature and the conditions of human existence against which the poem should be read. In addition it helps project the assumption that the king is the father of his subjects. He treats them with the mercy and love of a father, and in return they owe him gratitude, loyalty, trust, and obedience.

52

The treason of Absalom symbolizes the very personal nature of treason and rebellion. The parallel with the Father in Heaven ties this concept to the underlying religious imagery of the poem.

The images and allusions of the poem are in themselves an extensive field for analysis and study. In addition to the religious and filial allusions, though, the animal imagery recurs so often that it reveals with great skill the poet's concept of those opposing the king. This motif provides a significant gloss on the Jews' notion that "all but Savages were Slaves." The most frequent image refers to the serpent, and here again there is a clear relation to the poem's religious imagery. Corah is likened to the brazen serpent, the poet speaks of Achitophel's venom, and the king predicts that the witnesses will swear against each other "Till Viper-like their Mother Plot they tear." There are others such as the Levites being compared to a herd of animals, bull-faced Jonas, and even Achitophel's son, "that unfeather'd, two Leg'd thing." Animal imagery carries with it notions of lack of restraint, nature's state, ruthless self-interest, and ingratitude. It gains in significance as it contrasts to the religious symbolism of mercy and love.

Finally, the recurrent use of antithesis and contrast is of great importance. Its appropriateness in particular places has already been commented on. Its particular uses suggest that as a motif in the poem it symbolizes such things as the contrast between what man is and what he appears to be, between what he should be and what he is, between his own selfish actions and the forgiving mercy of those set above him. Man is composed of contending qualities. Even when he falls he may commit a godlike sin.

Absalom and Achitophel is a poem written in the past in terms appropriate to the poet's contemporaries. In order to understand the poet's meaning, the modern reader needs the help especially of the student of language and of the historian of ideas. But as a great poem it belongs to the present as well as the past. Historians may show how it was read by the poet's contemporaries, but it is a mere artifact unless it speaks directly and authentically to its modern reader.

Hudibras and the Nature of Man

The critical consensus about *Hudibras* is a paradox. Everyone agrees that there is greatness in the poem, but not many critics have found it. One critic classifies Butler as a "primitive," another comments on his "lack of psychological insight," and still another makes a special point of noting that Butler's personal view of society and man transcends the limits of *Hudibras.* Only one critic is comprehensive in dealing with *Hudibras* as a work of art, Ellen D. Leyburn in *Satiric Allegory: Mirror of Man,* a perceptive and stimulating discussion.[1] The one virtue that is generally agreed on is Butler's use of language or, as some term it, his wit. But it is also agreed that this virtue is localized. The poem is too long. There is too much conversation. It lacks coherence. As an attack on Puritans it is amusing, but it is overdone.

This chapter dissents. In *Hudibras* Butler has created a major poem which is not so much a comment on life as an expression by the poet of his conception of the nature of man and of the relation between man and man and between man and woman. The undue concern of many critics with the "objects" of Butler's satire has led them into a misreading of the poem and to a most unfortunate underreading as well. The common assumption that it is not a violence to Butler's purpose to discuss his language and wit without reference to the central purposes of the poem is a good example of underreading. *Hudibras* deserves the respect due any work of art: to be examined for itself rather than for its relation to historical events, literary history, the history of ideas, or the history of the author's thought. Of course, perceptive criticism has been written on Butler and his poem. The best single work on Butler is Ricardo Quintana's "Samuel Butler: A Restoration Figure in a Modern Light."[2] The best single criticism of the poem is contained in Ellen D. Leyburn's book. An earlier work of much value is Daniel Gibson's "Samuel Butler."[3]

Before discussing *Hudibras,* some answer should be made to the question, "What is the poem?" It was first published in three parts, and most critics regard all three parts together as "the poem." This is, of course, a legitimate way of looking at the work. It has, as a matter of record, the support of the *New English Dictionary.* However, it is also a matter of record that this way of looking at the poem has been unfruitful as far as form is concerned. Dr. Johnson, to cite the most eminent example, regarded the poem as incomplete and thought that even if it had been finished "there could only have been a succession of incidents, each of which might have happened without the rest, and which could not all co-operate to any single conclusion."[4] It seems wise, therefore, to try another approach that might yield more to the reader.

The position of most writers on the relation of the three parts is not stated explicitly, but it is nonetheless clear. They regard *Hudibras* as a long, continuously unfolding series of adventures. But this view obscures the way Butler published the poem. Part I is dated 1663; Part II, 1664; and Part III, 1678. Pepys purchased a copy on December 26, 1662. It read "*Hudibras, the first part.*" The crux is in the meaning of the word *part.* If it means an uncompleted portion, the breaks between the three parts can safely be ignored. But this is not the conception of the poem adopted here. The breaks between Parts I and II and between II and III are not arbitrary; rather they reflect a significant change in Hudibras the character and the values he holds and represents. The evidence for this conception will develop as the work itself is discussed. The chief critical result of the old view of "the whole poem" has been to encourage critics to make generalizations about Parts I, II, and III from observations made in Part I. Such generalizations have obscured the real nature of the development of *Hudibras.*

PART I

The constant emphasis upon the anti-Puritanism of *Hudibras,* the necessity for explaining contemporary allusions, and the trying and detailed efforts to identify real people in the poem have all tended to emphasize the contemporaneousness and the immediate apparent satiric objectives of Part I. It has been decoded, dated, and annotated, all of which is certainly the legitimate province of the literary historian. Such activity tends, however, to give a warped conception of the poem as a product of the imagination, for it leaves the impression that once the political situation has been explained the work of art has somehow been made clear. So few critics have worked with the poem itself that a number of crucial questions remain unanswered. One stands out above all others: What is the significance of the mock epic or mock romance of *Hudibras?* Why is Hudibras *Sir* Hudibras? What is the justification for mixing the anti-heroic and the anti-Puritan?

That Hudibras is both a Presbyterian and a knight errant should have aroused a great deal of comment. The usual explanation seems tacit. Hudibras was based upon Sir Henry Rosewell or Sir Samuel Luke; he must therefore be a knight. Since he is a knight, it is logical for him to engage in chivalric episodes. But such an answer should satisfy no one who has respect for Butler as an artist. A serious critic of the poem should comment, for a Presbyterian hero of romance requires admiration if nothing more.

The anti-heroic applied to the Presbyterians makes sense only as they are reformers, as they are the church militant. In that respect there is a grain of truth in the Presbyterian knight. But the hero of romance—and Sir Hudibras is that—has accepted a personal, heroic ideal which separates him from the religious "fanatic." Only one group in Butler's culture did accept the heroic ideal. The Cavaliers, not the Presbyterians, read the French romances. The Cavaliers, not the Presbyterians, held to the ideal of personal honor. They were the dashing heroes of the Civil Wars. Yet in spite of these ideals many of their number were corrupt, selfish, and cynical. And their heroism was futile and meaningless when measured practically. None of the Cavaliers saw himself in *Hudibras,* but then the Cavaliers were as serenely self-deceived as Hudibras himself.

It would be crude to say that the Cavaliers are an object of satire in the poem. This very denial is a measure of the way *Hudibras* has been warped by an historical interpretation. If the poem is looked at as an expression in poetic form of some sort of value or meaning which the author feels or has experienced, we will no longer be confronted by the black beasts of literalness and historicity. Looked at as an imaginative creation made out of the author's experience, Sir Hudibras can be seen as possessing characteristics of groups on both sides of the great social struggle. On this level he is not a representative of either group, for he is not an allegory. He expresses something that is not exclusive to either group but can be identified with both. Hudibras, whether the author is making the conscious effort or not, is able to express a feeling about man and society that is appropriate for all groups. If Hudibras has his birth partly as a result of this feeling, he is no longer inexplicable, for he is an anomaly only so long as we insist upon one "object" for Butler's satire, the Presbyterians.

Butler's ability to bring together disparate elements consciously can be illustrated on a less spectacular scale in the description of Hudibras. Hudibras does not cut his beard since he has vowed to let it grow until monarchy falls.

But when the State shall hap to reel,
'Twas to submit to fatal Steel,
And fall, as it was consecrate,
A Sacrifice to Fall of State. (I, i, p. 10)[5]

Hudibras is a Presbyterian, but Butler has borrowed the beard and oath from Phillip Nye, one of the dissenting brethren who opposed Presbyterian doctrines in the Assembly of Divines. In religious fanaticism, Butler sees there are no important differences between the sects. Hudibras is an object of religious satire, but Butler makes him something more than that, giving the character and the poem meaning and relevance for man and society as well as for one segment of that society. Hudibras has wider and more general significance than Butler has been given credit for. The anti-heroic is plot and fun, but what it signifies is also an essential part of the poem's accomplishment.

The anti-heroicism of *Hudibras* is almost always discussed in terms of the mocking of epical conventions and cliches as well as in terms of the "low" language and distorted rimes. Such discussions from this point of view must inevitably be inadequate, for they assume that the language of *Hudibras* is a device imposed from the outside. It is a good deal more than that. It is a symptom and essential technique which depends entirely upon the assumptions of the poem. These assumptions grow out of the values which the poet is giving expression to. This poem is no mere literary exercise like John Philip's Miltonic parody, the *Splendid Shilling*. Though we cannot say at any point that this is what Butler thought —or thought he thought—we can say that the poet has created a man and society that has consistency and satiric validity. The assumption of the anti-heroic is basic in that creation.

Although the poet's point of view is consistently anti-heroic, he must adjust his technique to his materials. Material which the heroic point of view would regard as "low" is treated ironically.

The upright *Cerdon* next advanc't
Of all his Race the Valiant'st;
Cerdon the Great, renown'd in Song,
Like Herc'les for repair of wrong. (I, ii. p. 39)

Matters that the heroic point of view would regard as highly valuable may be associated with material the heroic point of view looks down on

> In *Mathematicks* he was greater
> Than *Tycho Brahe,* or *Erra Pater*:
> For he, by *Geometrick* scale,
> Could take the size of *Pots* of *Ale* (I, i, p. 6)

Sometimes Butler relies on straight realism

> He thrust his Hand into his Hose,
> And found both by his Eyes and Nose,
> 'Twas only Choler, and not Bloud,
> That from his wounded Body flow'd. (I, iii, p. 76)

The basic irony of Part I is the interplay between the points of view of author and character.

But what does the anti-heroic lead to in the poem? Professors Quintana and Leyburn subsume Hudibras' anti-heroic actions under the term *grotesque,* and regard that quality as functional in the poem. Quintana calls the grotesque "a conceptual device by means of which the ordered world of reason, where all illusions have been dispelled by the intellect, is affirmed."[6] Miss Leyburn says: "Butler's artistic point of view is perfectly consistent: it is an angle of vision that creates steady distortion and persistently reveals the perverted human mind that he scorns."[7]

The grotesque does perform a philosophical and at the same time aesthetic function in the poem, but the reader cannot assume that the criterion against which it must be judged is a proper, attainable norm of human behavior. At the risk of oversimplifying, the critical problem which the grotesque presents can be reduced to alternative questions: Is Butler implying that Hudibras has deviated from a code of conduct which—though perhaps not attainable in its ideal form—can and ought to be followed by all men? or Is *Hudibras* a poem which by satiric exaggeration emphasizes that ideals of human conduct are mere pretense, having no relationship to man's actual nature, which is foolish, selfish, and immoral?

Butler's technique obscures the answer somewhat. In most satires the false view is represented by the satirized object, and the poet, by one means or another, states or implies the "right" view. This right view is almost always a simple, moral assumption that is easily accepted: All men should act reasonably, for example. But Butler does not soothe his readers with a platitude. *Hudibras* has two points of view, the author's and Hudibras'. In Part I, at least, Hudibras' view is consistently heroic. His basic assumptions are probably very close to most of the readers', though his eccentricities tend to make his heroic values more obvious than they are in most people. He has personal, religious, and social ideals which he is willing to act upon. His belief in human reason is complete. When he cannot live up to his ideals, he rationalizes rather than abandon them.

The point of view of the author, on the other hand, is just as consistently anti-heroic. Hudibras is denigrated—with increasing bitterness as the poem progresses—and the poet gives no hint that anyone in the poem might live up to any sort of heroic ideal. There are no "good" characters, and the poem emphasizes the discrepancy between what Hudibras is and what he thinks he is or pretends to be. The reader may believe it possible for man to live by heroic values, but there is no evidence in the poem that its author thinks so.

Author and reader condemn the values of Hudibras, but those who look from the poem to a world of ordered reason take one more step than the work itself justifies. They assume that Butler is using Hudibras as an extreme example and that it is the extravagance of his heroic assumptions rather than the assumptions themselves that Butler is emphasizing. From this assumption it inevitably follows that Butler would be willing to accept the ideals of Hudibras if they were not stated in an extreme form. Neither this assumption nor its consequence can be shown to be valid for the poem. The fact that the poet gives no such authorization is in itself significant; so is the fact that this assumption is more typical of one who holds Hudibras' point of view than one who agrees with the poet. Since this notion leads to a perversion of the presented values of the poem, it ought to be rejected. The anti-heroic is basic in the poet's conception, not just a technique. The contrast in values is between what Hudibras thinks he is and what the poet shows him to be, not between what Hudibras is and the proper mind of man.

Butler's anti-heroic assumptions are nowhere clearer than in his language. It has, of course, always been quoted approvingly, but often without a demonstration of a full understanding of its greatness. Anyone who can analyze the language without reference to the purpose of the poem sees through the glass darkly. The notion that this is mere rollicking doggerel is, as most would agree generally, utterly false. The poem could have been written, as Dr. Johnson pointed out, only by a man of great learning and great observation. The language shows the highest degree of sophistication, which in a work of art should not be equated to elegance. One of the very interesting points to be noted in examining the language is how much relatively is devoted to demolishing the heroic assumptions of the character and how little, in comparison to the widespread impression, to religious fanaticism.

Some of Butler's language is direct denunciation, as his lines on the *New Light* are.

> 'Tis a *Dark-Lanthorn* of the Spirit,
> Which none see by but those that bear it.
> A Light that falls down from on high,
> For Spiritual Trades to couzen by:
> An *Ignis Fatuus* that bewitches,
> And leads Men into Pools and Ditches,
> To make them *dip* themselves, and sound
> For Christendom [in] dirty Pond;
> To dive like Wild-foul for Salvation,
> And fish to catch Regeneration. (I, i, p. 16)

This passage is characteristic of Butler. The three brilliant figures of light give an impression almost of improvisation. But they are not random. The first figure—"*Dark-Lanthorn*"—carries the implication of theft, the second—"to couzen by"— a direct statement of knavery following an ironic reference to the self-designated saints. The third reference—to false fire—ties the falseness and knavery to the Anabaptists' religious practices, at the same time making an ironic reference to the sectarians as fishers, though instead of fishers of men Butler calls them *Wild-foul*. Seen as a pun, this term fits physically and morally as a description of men who have been led into pools and ditches. This is a splendid passage, and surely the humor and jingle in it are only contributing qualities.

Usually, however, Butler depends upon indirection rather than straightforward denunciation. The homely term is a frequent means of attacking the heroic. It is, of course, a device that usually produces humor.

> This said, the high outrageous mettle
> Of *Knight* began to cool and settle. (I, iii, p. 56)

Puns are used the same way:

> The trenchant blade, *Toledo* trusty,

For want of fighting was grown rusty,
And eat into it self, for lack
Of some body to hew and hack. (I, i, p. 12)

The figurative use of eat takes on a literal meaning in the midst
of vittles and eating. This literal hunger of the sword is brought
out in the rest of the passage:

The peaceful Scabbard where it dwelt,
The Rancor of its Edge had felt:
For of the lower end two handful,
It had devoured 'twas so manful (I, i, pp. 12–13)

The scabbard is even measured in handfuls.

Though this does not pretend to the sort of analysis Butler's
language has so long deserved, two more anti-heroic strategies
should be especially noted. One is Butler's trick of turning an
abstract quality, sometimes a spiritual one, into something tangible
and concrete. This is the philosopher's stone with a vengeance, for
it turns pure gold to lead.

By help of these (as he profest)
He had *First Matter* seen undrest:
He took her naked all alone,
Before one Rag of *Form* was on. (I, i, pp. 17–18)

Or

He could raise Scruples dark and nice,
And after solve 'em in a trice:
As if Divinity had catch'd
The Itch, of purpose to be scratch'd (I, i, p. 7)

The effect of these is to indicate the inadequacy of Ralph's understanding and the lack, in Hudibras, of a serious intellectual or
emotional purpose.

The other use of language is the allusion. This is a thorny subject because the kinds of allusions, the frequency, and the application vary from one canto to another. The sort that is of particular
interest here is that in which the allusion has its heroic qualities
reduced by being compared to an obviously unheroic situation in
Hudibras. The tendency of many of these is not to emphasize the
difference between a low situation in *Hudibras* and a heroic one
outside the poem. The tendency is to degrade the heroic allusion
itself by showing how it is like the low thing or situation in the
poem.

61

Sturdy he was, and no less able
Than *Hercules* to cleanse a stable (I. ii, p. 4)

For as *Achilles* dipt in Pond,
Was *Anabaptized* free from wound (I, iii, p. 63)

When *Orsin* first let fly a stone
At *Ralpho;* not so huge a one
As that which *Diomed* did maul
Aeneas on the Bum withal (I, iii, p. 72)

These allusions and others like them attack the heroic beyond the limits of *Hudibras*. In effect, Butler is putting the heroes of antiquity into the same category with Hudibras. He shows here not a mere trick of language, but a philosophical assumption.

But what of the language of Hudibras himself. With some reservations it can be called rather consistently heroic. (The speech to the rabble in Canto II of Part I is exceptional on several counts.) It reflects rather accurately what Hudibras feels, and Hudibras feels like a hero. If this were a normal mock heroic, the poet would "elevate" a "low" subject, which is what Butler does with the bear baiters. For the most part Hudibras retains his own heroic outlook and the irony lies in the discrepancies between his point of view and the poet's.

The rimes of *Hudibras* grow out of the same assumptions, but there is so little factual information on the rimes that it would be futile to discuss them in detail unless they had been examined with care. Many of the easy generalities about Butler's twisted rimes are obviously wrong. Most of his riming is true, though the sounds were based on actual pronunciation—sometimes variant pronunciations—rather than on spelling. Dryden's work is so available that he may well represent our concept of the late seventeenth-century standard. But Dryden's insistence upon agreement of spelling as well as pronunciation—his "correctness"—is rather uncommon. Butler should rather be compared to John Oldham, who is also misjudged in this respect. Without digressing to offer linguistic evidence, one might suggest that Butler's strained rimes depend upon a slight shift in stress and juncture rather than upon mispronunciation of sounds.

For Butler language is a great and subtle instrument through which he presents a conception of man. Like any poetic language its effectiveness depends upon an integral relation with the material presented and the author's assumptions. And it should be examined like any other poetic language, not as an interminable series of jabs and stabs or anti-Puritan thumps.

Satiric narrative usually has more symbolic than literal meaning. Considered as an entity, the first part has demonstrable and adequate narrative coherence. Canto I contains the descriptions of Hudibras and Ralph, their sighting of the crowd, and their consequent discussion of bear baiting, which is interrupted. Canto II has the descriptions of the enemy heroes and heroine and the account of the first battle, which ends in the defeat of Hudibras' enemies and the imprisonment of Crowdero. Canto III contains the rallying of the crowd; the second battle, which ends in the defeat of Hudibras and Ralph by Trulla; the imprisonment of Hudibras and Ralph; and, finally, the resumed discussion between the two in which Ralph tries to prove that synods are mystical bear gardens.

The action comes after the description of the main characters—D'Avenant used the same procedure in *Gondibert*—and once it has begun it unfolds as single, complete, and of a certain magnitude. The plot itself is ironic, for the conventional lines of plot development have been reversed. If Hudibras were a normal hero he would arouse the fears of his readers by facing almost certain defeat, then vindicate their heroic assumptions about him by utterly defeating the enemy in a second engagement. But Hudibras suffers from his alliance with an unsympathetic poet. Instead of losing the first battle, Hudibras wins. The second battle, which he should win, he loses. These battles, it should be said, are notable more for their realism than for their more widely reputed exaggeration or distortion, though the language in which they are described, especially in the second canto, is often heightened.

> The Gun went off: and as it was
> Still fatal to stout *Hudibras*,
> In all his feats of Arms, when least
> He dreamt of it to prosper best;
> So now he far'd, the shot let fly
> At randome 'mong the Enemy,
> Pierc'd *Talgol*'s Gabberdine, and grazing
> Upon his Shoulder, in the passing
> Lodg'd in *Magnano*'s brass Habergeon,
> Who straight *a Surgeon* cry'd, *a Surgeon*.
> He tumbled down, and as he fell,

Did *Murther, murther, murther* yell.
This startled their whole Body so,
That if the *Knight* had not let go
His Arms, but been in warlike plight,
H' had won (the second time the fight.)
As if the *Squire* had but fal'n on,
He had inevitably done:
But he diverted with the care
Of *Hudibras* his wound forbare
To press th' advantage of his fortune,
While danger did the rest dishearten. (I, iii, p. 73)

But even in defeat Hudibras cannot be a sympathetic character. The final scene of Hudibras and Ralph in the stocks debating the proposition that synods are mystical bear gardens furnishes the ironic plot with a resounding anticlimax. The end is a trailing off rather than a conclusion.

Any broader view of *Hudibras* has implications for the character Ralph. He is, of course, a prime part of the propagandistic function of the poem. But even after he has been called an Independent, a good deal remains to be said. Ralph has two great interests—logic and religion—which he manages to combine. These are not mean interests as such. Most of Butler's contemporaries would probably have agreed that religion and reason were God's greatest gifts to man. Why, then, is Ralph a humorous, unsympathetic character?

Ralph appears in three different lights in the poem: (1) in the description of Canto I; (2) in the battles of Cantos II and III; and (3) in the debates of Cantos I and III. In the description of Canto I, the poet deals most unsympathetically with Ralph's "Gifts" and sectarianism. He is treated with scorn as both short-witted and superstitious. Over half the description is devoted to Ralph's "mystick Learning," though it is not used at all later in the poem. This description is sharply at variance with Ralph as we see him in the battles. He is humorous, it is true, but he also gives Hudibras wise advice. In the battles he is thoroughly sympathetic.

Quoth *Ralph,* How great I do not know
We may by being beaten grow;
But none that see how here we sit
Will judge us overgrown with Wit. (I, iii, 86)

The description of Canto I is also at variance with Ralph the debater, for Ralph is brilliant in argument, at least if one accepts Biblical proofs. The proposition which he defends is not orthodox divinity: all synods are mystical bear gardens. It is, however, exactly right for Butler's purposes. If Ralph proves it, Butler makes a point. But the proposition is bizarre enough to give the whole serious proceeding an air of insanity. The atmosphere, however, should not obscure Ralph's excellent arguments. His analogy between Presbyterianism and Roman Catholicism can hardly be called nonsense by those who nod approvingly over Milton's "new presbyter is old priest writ large."

> *Presbytery* does but translate
> The Papacy to a *Free State*,
> A *Commonwealth of Popery*,
> Where ev'ry Village is a *See*
> As well as *Rome*, and must maintain
> A *Tithe Pig Metropolitane:*
> Where ev'ry *Presbyter* and *Deacon*
> Commands the *Keys* for Cheese and Bacon;
> And ev'ry Hamlet's governed
> By's *Holiness*, the *Church's Head*,
> More haughty and severe in's place
> Than *Gregory* and *Boniface*.

Ralph as the poet describes him and Ralph as the poet presents him is not wholly consistent.

The discrepancy can be looked upon as proof of a failure on the part of the poet to create a consistent character. Possibly this explanation would be accepted as the poet's conscious intent. But it avoids the crux, which is explaining why Butler would allow this inconsistency to exist, for it is, after all, difficult to maintain that Butler would write something he did not think made sense. A more logical position is that the description of Ralph and the actions of Ralph are both of them views held by Butler.

Butler's attitude toward Ralph, as we see it in the poem, is ambivalent. The fact that the views are apparently contradictory does not mean that each cannot have validity, for of course each can. But what is it in Ralph that the poet admires and scorns? It is certainly not the humane nature of Ralph's religion, for the characters in the poem regard religion as a series of tenets rather than a way of life. It is not Ralph's Independency, for this sect is ridiculed. The place Ralph is treated gentlest is in the exercise of reason. By seventeenth century standards his attack on synods was well handled. Though Ralph defends *Light* and *Gifts*, he does not depend on them. After Hudibras offers his thin and ironically self defeating arguments, Ralph is given the lines attacking learning.

> Quoth *Ralpho*, Nothing but th'abuse
> Of *Humane Learning* you produce;
> *Learning* that Cobweb of the Brain,
> *Profane,* erronius, and vain;
> A trade of knowledge as repleat
> As others are with fraud and cheat;
> An Art t'encumber *Gifts* and *Wit*,
> And render both for nothing fit; (I, iii, p. 94)

> For nothing goes for *Sense* or *Light*
> That will not with old rules jump right.
> As if Rules were not in the Schools
> Deriv'd from Truth, but Truth from Rules.

> This *Pagan, Heathenish* invention
> Is good for nothing but Contention.
> For as in Sword-and-Buckler Fight,
> All blows do on the Target light:
> So when Men argue, the great'st part
> O' the Contest falls on terms of Art,
> Until the Fustian stuff be spent,
> And then they fall to the' Argument. (I, iii, p. 94)

This is not altogether fool. But since Ralph's technique of argument is the same as Hudibras'—it is just a better argument—this comment leads to distrust of all argument. The ambivalence, then, would seem to lie in a favorable attitude toward reason, an attitude whic hcould be deduced from the well-made argument presented sympathetically, and an unfavorable attitude toward that same process of reason as shown in Ralph's attack on learning. The man himself is described as a short-witted, superstitious near-knave. This attitude toward Ralph refutes the notion that Butler is attacking only the abuse of reason. Of course he is attacking the extreme. But in drawing Ralph as he has, he seems to be directing his distrust at reason itself. Admittedly there is something to be said on both sides, but whichever side is taken Ralph must no longer be looked upon as merely a ridiculous representative of a Puritan sect. He has become a means by which Butler has expressed his value of the rational process. In addition, the ambivalence of Butler's attitude toward this character helps show that he is not a simple counter moved about in jest.

Hudibras is composed of the Puritan and the heroic, qualities that would adequately symbolize completeness at the time *Hudibras* was written. He is a man obsessed by religion and by a point of view. He rationalizes, and his love for the widow is not untainted by self-interest, but he should not be called a rogue. Though he poet presents Ralph as something of a cheat, his emphasis with Hudibras is chiefly on the anti-heroic. Perhaps this is why *Hudibras,* Part I, is innocent rather than bitter. Hudibras' misconception grows out of naïveté rather than evil. The laughter is still devastating, though neither Ralph nor Hudibrac is made obnoxious morally. But of course Hudibras' misconception of himself is so fundamental that it antedates morals.

PART II

The second part is not a mere extension of the first, though the two are joined by continuation of action and characters. The subject is different, the characters show a new conception, and the poet's technique has changed. The time of the poem shifts from the early days of the Civil Wars to a period at least as late as the Commonwealth. Although Hudibras is not through with battle, he is no longer primarily a soldier, and in dropping this role he drops many of the heroic attitudes of the first part. The main subject of the first two cantos is love; the whole action depends upon it. Unlike Hudibras' earlier obsessions, this one is selfish; his attitude is cynical. Part II is not pleasant and light; it is peopled by knaves.

The moral character of Hudibras degenerates as Part II proceeds. In Canto I his love for the widow is shown to be a feigned passion motivated by selfish, material motives.

> I do confess, with Goods and Land,
> I'd have a Wife, at second hand;
> And such you are: nor is't your person,
> My stomach's set so *sharp*, and fierce on,
> But 'tis (your better part) your *Riches,*
> That my enamour'd heart bewitches. (II, i, p. 117).

His lack of moral fiber is further revealed in Canto II as he and Ralph decide to swear that he has been whipped even though he has not. Finally, at the end of Canto III he acts the part of thief, coward, and treacherous friend.

This change in Hudibras has important consequences. It means an end of a sustained attempt at the mock heroic, for there is no longer an heroic character to mock. Although the poet's assumptions in the second part may not be essentially different from those of the first, there are elements of bitterness and misanthropy which are new. Whether Part II should be called cynical or realistic depends largely upon the reader's own assumptions about man, but the world Butler presents is a world of knavery and broken faith. Love is in great part his topic, and a writer's attitude toward love can be used as an indication of his assumptions about man. Love before marriage can be seen in Hudibras and the widow; love after marriage in the skimmington ride. Although neither state conforms to a romantic conception of ideal love, Butler may have regarded them as more accurate statements of actual human values. The parody of romantic debates on love is very likely an expression of Butler's disgust with the pretense of the romantic ideal.

Butler's use of love as the key issue of Part II allows Hudibras to retain a universality. Religion, as it did in Part I, demonstrates qualities of mind. Love is used to demonstrate Hudibras' point of view, no longer naively heroic but now meanly selfish. If Hudibras is only a vehicle for religious satire, he is grossly eccentric and amusing. But if we take him as Butler's way of saying something about man, he becomes serious; indeed he becomes at the same time funny and profoundly discouraging. Butler's use of Sidrophel raises a number of interesting artistic problems. It is enough here to say that as it does deal with the supernatural, astrology is an obvious field to harbor fraud and pretense. In the poem it serves as a parallel to, perhaps substitute for, religion.

The change apparent in Hudibras also leads to a significant change in technique. No longer do we have the parallel, conflicting points of view with Hudibras supporting the heroic and the poet the anti-heroic. Hudibras is no longer capable of heroic assumptions. He is a fraud and cheat, and he recognizes it. There is, then, but one point of view toward Hudibras and, by extension, toward the way men act. This shift away from the heroic has its effect upon the language of this part. There is very little discrepancy between the language of the poet and that of the characters, for they all look at life in the same way. There seem to be fewer allusions to the great men of antiquity, and probably fewer altogether, though the occurrence of allusions varies from place to place.

The change in Hudibras also leads to an end to innocent laughter. The new Hudibras is a conscious villain, and even as we laugh there is a tinge of disillusion or disappointment. The reader with heroic impulses no longer has anything in common with the "hero." This new-found discouragement carries with it the feeling that there is no moral hope for Hudibras. Insofar as *Hudibras* can be generalized, this world created by Butler is one without real hope of moral improvement. The kind of degradation imposed on Ralph makes this point neatly. In Part I Ralph was in places given gentle treatment. Butler did have some admiration, however reluctant and temporary, for the power of reason. In Part II, the assumption is different. Man is selfish, willing to follow his own advantage. Reason is corruptible, ready to prove whatever the will of man wishes. What Hudibras desires, Ralph can prove.

If we take the pattern of characterization of this part as something more than merely perfunctory, we can only say that it seems to reflect not so much a sense of the anti-heroic as a recognition of the pretense of human conduct. Hudibras is the winner at the end of Part II, but he wins at the expense of all moral principle. The debates that take place in each canto can have no issue in truth for the debaters themselves are frauds and cheats. This part is notable for insincere debate and self-defeating action. While it may be true that the action of Part II would be inadequate for an epic or romance, it is more appropriate for this poem if it is considered symbolically. Hudibras wins twice during the three cantos. His first triumph is an intellectual one in which he (as he thinks) outwits the widow by finding a way out of his whipping. This first victory is a fraudulent self-deception gained at the expense of personal intellectual honesty. The second victory, over Sidrophel and Whachum, is one from which he flees in fear, leaving his squire Ralph to take the blame. This latter victory demonstrates his lack of honor and integrity. Both actions grow out of the same qualities in Hudibras, but they are complementary in that the first is shown by the poet as primarily a failure of personal integrity; the second is more obviously social in that it shows his failure to fulfill what he owes to Ralph.

Part II shows a bitter change. The feelings that dominate the characters are mean, selfish, and dishonest. Nor is this represented as a deviation from normal, human conduct, for the poet agrees that this is human nature.

PART III

The change from Part I to Part II was sharp, but the transition from II to III is much easier. The third and last part is tied to the preceding canto by similarities in technique, language, conception of the characters, and action. Only in form, in the inclusion of a middle canto on a topic outside the "plot" of *Hudibras,* is there striking change.

Part III is the degradation of Hudibras. He is a thieving, lying, canting, superstitious fool. He is contemptible, and the laughter which he inspires is altogether unsympathetic. The subject of love is concluded in Canto I as the widow and Hudibras debate the condition of marriage. The widow argues that the woman's fortune is the only object of love.

> To that alone the Bridegroom's wedded,
> The Bride a Flam that's superseded.
> To that their Faith is still made good,
> And all the Oaths to us they vow'd.
> For when we once resign our Pow'rs,
> W' have nothing left we can call ours.
> Our Money's now become the Miss,
> Of all your Lives and Services;
> And we forsaken, and Post-pon'd,
> But Bawds to what before we own'd.
> Which as it made y' at first Gallant us,
> So now hires others to supplant us. (III, i, p. 222)

Hudibras' arguments are either obviously false or self-defeating. Not much is made of Hudibras' religion in the first canto, though it is made the basis of the baffled knight's final, degrading confession. The "spirit" questions him for almost fifty lines.

> What's Orthodox and true Believing
> Against a Conscience?—A good Living.
> What makes Rebelling against Kings
> A Good Old Cause? Administrings.
> What makes all Doctrines plain and clear?
> About Two hundred pounds a year.
> And that which was prov'd true before,
> Prove false again? Two hundred more. (III, i, pp. 229–230)

If there were any justice in Hudibras' position, the satire on the law in Canto III would lose a good deal of its bite. *Hudibras* has been called unfinished, but that is because the critics have looked only at the action. The title page indicates this is the last part. It is. But the finality lies in the character of Hudibras rather than in the accumulation of incident. The heroic point of view has been degraded and discredited. There remains nothing new for Hudibras to do. The poet has made his point.

Canto II is a digression from the adventures of Hudibras. Although it raises a number of interesting questions, none of them are germane to this discussion.

The third canto of Part III, the canto on the law, closing with the epistles of Hudibras and the widow, is more conventional in its subject matter and more obviously not directed toward the Puritans. It is significant to an interpretation of the poem in that it adds law and the courts to the other objects of satire. The counsellor is a villain of the same stamp as Hudibras. Once again we cannot conclude that because he is evil he is an example of a deviation from some human norm. Indeed, appearance is in favor of taking the lawyer as satirically representative of actual human values. The poet's description of justice implies there are no others.

Butler concludes this third and last part with two verse epistles, *"An Heroical Epistle of* Hudibras *to his Lady"* and "The Lady's Answer To The Knight." The subject is love, and they give the final view of Hudibras. It is an ugly, repulsive view of a man who is selfish, deceitful, and stupid.

Viewed in its three successive parts, *Hudibras* is a poem about the nothingness of human ideals. They are pretenses to which human conduct gives the lie. Those who see the poem as merely anti-Puritan satire strip it of its greatest achievement, for its greatness lies in what it says about man. To state the values of the poem is to judge them, for they can be formulated only in terms of the values as religion, love, honor, self-knowledge, friendship, reason, cynical despair. To others it may be an honest satiric appraisal of the state of man, unflinching in the courage of its realism. Dealing as it does with a fundamental view of life, touching as themes such values as religion, love, honor, self knowledge, friendship, reason, superstition, and justice, this great poem reaches to the heart of the human condition. It is hard to believe that some critics are merely amused.

Arbuthnot's Simple Plan

Pope's *Epistle to Dr. Arbuthnot* has experienced the vicissitudes of criticism. Critics have been delighted, shocked, and coldly objective in its presence. Doubtless scholars of the future will continue to add to the store of thoughtful, perceptive commentary, but it is unlikely they will devise a new "right" interpretation that will reveal a different poem from the one we read today.

Modern criticism is dominated by two very different ways of looking at the poem: the biographical and the aesthetic. Pope's own "Advertisement" before the poem gives ample evidence that he regarded the epistle as a personal defense against his detractors. Earlier readers usually took his words literally, and this concept of the poem as propaganda can still be traced in most modern critics. Some writers on Pope still read the poem for its "factual" value:

> Pope has given us a radiant picture of his father in the *Epistle to Arbuthnot.* The portrait which emerges is more admirable for its integrity than for any fancy touches Pope might have intended in praise of his lineage. From the testimony of those who knew the family, Pope's portrait of his father was both real and accurate.[1]

The aesthetic point of view takes no cognizance of biographical material as such. Miss Rebecca Parkin, though she sees in the poem many similarities to Pope's life remarks of the persona:

> Notwithstanding, the protagonist of this poem is dramatically not autobiographically conceived. The coincidence of certain traits and circumstances of the dramatic character with Pope's biography has nothing to do with the success of the poem as a poem. These traits are used dramatically, as an objective element in the work, to create a well-defined genre pose. The Horatian pose of the injured but superior poet is as fixed and objective as the pose of the Petrarchan sonneteer.[2]

Most critics combine these two views. They see Pope writing from personal motivation and associate the personal satire of the poem, especially the characters of Atticus and Sporus, with contemporaries. But they go on to comment upon the aesthetic development of the poem without maintaining that the poem is accurate biography. One of the good commentators on the *Epistle to Dr. Arbuthnot*, Robert W. Rogers, shows this dual view in finding two purposes of the poem.

One objective is to justify the conduct of Alexander Pope in the face of charges leveled at him by his critics . . . . But the poem is more than an apologia: it is a study of the character and conduct proper to a successful writer. The picture in it of reasonable patience with importunity, concern for merit, scorn of patronage, and humility in private life is a lecture to the times on the principles by which a literary man should live.[3]

Mr. Rogers shows that the aesthetic development of the poem can be described in terms of the three formal satirical characters—Atticus, Bufo, and Sporus. The discussion that follows identifies Atticus as Addison and Sporus as Lord Hervey, but it goes on to discuss in detail the values which each of the characters represents as well. This is no mere perfunctory annotation. It is an attempt to see the poem in terms of Alexander Pope the man and in terms of any satirist. The portrait of Pope is called idealized, not factual. There is, however, an underlying assumption of possible historical validity:

> In the character of Sporus Pope says nothing of Hervey that has not already been said. The aspects of Hervey's character featured in "Sporus," are for the most part true, and despicable.[4]

Atticus, Bufo, and Sporus have always dominated the poem. They are striking "characters," and they do play a prominent part in Pope's design. But a good deal of their prominence, at least so far as the critics are concerned, has been due to their historical associations. The identification of Atticus as Addison, a history of the lines, and an attempt to decide whether the lines are a just portrait of their original requires a concentration which, however well merited, tends to give Atticus a special importance in the poem. The remark so often met with that the lines on Sporus seem inspired by a special sort of hatred of Hervey seem subjectively *post hoc, propter hoc.* Any critic who tries to read the poem historically is almost sure to devote a large part of his commentary to these lines if only because there is so much tangible information available about them.

The three characters are, of course, vital parts of the poem, but the poem does not turn on them. The poem develops out of four contrasts, neither side of which is complete without the other. One of the characteristics of the satiric mode is the depiction of values

73

of which the poet disapproves. Explicit or implicit in the satiric work is the standard by which the poet judges. The poet's values are stated here so openly and for belief that there is an alternation of the satiric and non-satiric modes as well as a contrast in values. The significant structural pattern of the *Epistle to Dr. Arbuthnot* is the presentation of contrasting values, all of them stated by the poet in terms of Pope, his friends, and his enemies. The "plan" of the poem lies in the fact that each contrast deals with values of deeper significance than the last.

The poem begins in a comic vein (1–48).[5] The difficulties of the poet are amusing, for the confusion of divine madness and the more mundane sort does not, for the reader at least, violate any significant values. The very number of foolish, bad writers who solicit him makes all this serious to the poet—a civil, long-suffering man—but not for the reader, who at first feels no concern. As the poem progresses, however, the incidents begin to show malice and immorality. The actions of Pitholeon and the stranger (49–68) introduce this new significance. The fawning and the flattery of this host of nameless scribblers who beg for help they do not deserve provide the climax (109–124) of the satiric presentation. Opposed to this character-en-masse is the character of the poet. Stress is placed upon his writing and literary abilities, but neither here nor later is the literary considered without the moral. There is nothing mechanical about the contrast between the poet's own beginning and his suitors', but the parallels are drawn for anyone who looks. His native ability, his encouragement by men of taste, his unselfish motivation, his study, his humility, and his morality are drawn against the foil of the petty, vain scribblers. The transition (173–192) to the next part of the poem contains the significant observation that the bad qualities of these bad writers flow directly out of their moral deficiencies. Their unworthiness is compounded by their pride, two qualities that lead naturally to the sort of writing the poet contemns.

The character of Atticus follows as a part of the second contrast. This is a meaningful development for the poem, for Atticus has all the purely literary essentials for greatness. He is a genius and a gentleman, but his jealousy leads him to encourage wits and Templars and repress writers of talent. Atticus fails to play the part he has the genius for because he lacks the moral qualities a great writer needs. The character of the poet contrasts directly with that of Atticus. The development of the parallels indicates the poet thinks of himself as an equal of Atticus, not a possible member of the senate. The proud independence of the poet is a moral virtue. It also serves to introduce Bufo.

Pride is the moral failing of Bufo, and it corrupts his judgment just as jealousy had frustrated Atticus. Bufo is more reprehensible than Atticus, however, for his position and wealth give him a special responsibility which it is criminal to avoid.

> But still the Great have kindness in reserve,
> He helped to bury whom he helped to starve.

The contrast of the poet with Bufo is not so close as that with Atticus, though it is pointed (255–60) when the poet sets himself against the "Great" with their treatment of Gay as a criterion. Of course, the poet's pride in his independence contrasts to Bufo's pride, though we are really asked to draw a parallel between the poet and Dryden (245–46). The significant development in this section is the way moral values begin to take precedence over literary.

> Why am I asked what next shall see the light?
> Heav'ns! was I born for nothing but to write?
> Has Life no Joys for me? or (to be grave)
> Have I no Friend to serve, no Soul to save?

The poet does not say literature is unimportant, but he does say it comes only as a concomitant of other values which are important to him. The statement, which follows, of the subject of the poet's verse, indicates that the chief value of poetry is its moral effect. He rejects all writing that leads to the discomfiture of virtue. A denunciation of those who deliberately misread his lines and thus pervert a chief end of poetry leads directly into the character of Sporus.

The portrait of Sporus and the fourth character of the poet make the climax of the poem. Whatever Lord Hervey was, Sporus is not a court poet; there is nothing literary about him. His connection with the poet is his malicious, wholly unwarranted misreading of the poet's work. The malice of the man is directly attributable to his repulsive, immoral character. The poet's defense against misreading is to place Sporus' character against the poet's own. Sporus is the culmination, and more, of the bad values the poet has attacked through the first three contrasts. He is annoying, unintelligent, a proud, spiteful, jealous, ambitious fop. Against this disgusting, impotent, vile antithesis is set the poet with all his virtues. He is manly, honest, and moral, rejecting such immoralities as ambition, foppery, love of money, flattery, and either pride or servility. A moral man and moral poet, he attacks knavery wherever he finds it, though he has stood much in the cause of virtue. But why is Sporus the culmination? Why is he, as far as the poet is concerned, more important than a character like Atticus or Bufo? He can be properly understood only in the perspective of all four contrasts. The nameless bad writers, Atticus, and Bufo are chiefly responsible for creating bad poetry. They are also obstacles to a poet of real merit, though their discouragement might be chiefly indirect or through omission. But the evil actions of Sporus are directed at destroying the good poet and at perverting one of the chief ends of the poet's work.

> That Fop, whose pride affects a Patron's name,
> Yet absent, wounds an Author's honest fame:
> Who can your Merit selfishly approve,
> And show the Sense of it without the Love;
> Who has the Vanity to call you Friend,
> Yet wants the Honour injured to defend;
> Who tells whate'er you think, whate'er you say,
> And, if he lye not, must at least betray.

These actions are directed at blackening the poet's reputation, his other activity at blackening the poet's work.

> Who to the *Dean*, and *silver Bell* can swear,
> And sees at *Cannons* what was never there:
> Who reads, but with a Lust to mis-apply,
> Make Satire a Lampoon, and Fiction, Lye.

These are the most heinous offenses that can be committed against a writer or against poetry.

The poem does drop to a quieter note at the end, but it is not accurate to say that it ends on a domestic note, as though something new were being introduced. It is consistent with the developing values of the poem that the poet should show himself finally in the role of the faithful son, preserver of innocence, not as a successful, moral man of letters. By various poetic means Pope has asserted that in some sense bad writers are bad men, that immorality perverts literature. Men who encourage bad poets and attack good ones do so from moral failings. He does not maintain this condition is immutable; he only implies that there are no exceptions. Conversely, the good man and the good poet go together. It is, therefore, entirely fitting that the poem should close on a moral rather than literary note.

This has been called a personal poem; most commentators insist on this quality. Of course it is, in the sense that most great poems can be called personal: the poet uses his experience and transforms it. Many commentators, however, expend their energy on the raw material rather than on the experience transformed. Surely the best that can be said for such activity is that it is distracting. It is not in the nature of poetry to contain facts. It contains values. Take part of the description of the poet's father.

> Un-learned, he knew no Schoolman's subtle Art,
> No Language, but the Language of the Heart.
> By Nature honest, by Experience wise,
> Healthy by Tem'prance and by Exercise:
> His Life, tho' long, to sickness past unknown,
> His Death was instant, and without a groan.
> Oh grant me, thus to live, and thus to die!
> Who sprung from Kings shall know less joy than I.

This is not Alexander Pope's father, but a statement of the values for which the father stood in the poet's mind. This is the only condition under which the next-to-the-last line could have meaning. To live in a state of honest innocence, not to live the life of his father, is what the poet desires. Good poetry may not make bad biography as a matter of course, but it certainly makes for suspicion.

But what of the famous characters of Atticus and Sporus? To what extent are they personal and particular? The nature of poetry and the nature of human values foredooms an historic, personal reading of such satire to partial success at best. The case of Addison will illustrate.[6] The standard information about these lines is to the effect that the original of Atticus is Addison. These lines were written at an earlier date and, prior to the epistle, published. There then follows a discussion of the differences between Pope and Addison over politics and over rival translations of the *Iliad*. Behind the annotation on Atticus lie two assumptions. Both need examination.

First the annotator must assume that an objective knowledge of Joseph Addison, Alexander Pope, and their relationship will somehow make the poet's attitude toward Atticus more understandable to the reader. It allows, so the thinking goes, moderns to read the poem as one of Pope's contemporaries did. Actually, of course, the historical information only gives the illusion of the eighteenth-century point of view. The only reader who can feel the effect of identifying Atticus and Addison is one who sees Addison as a representative of some sort of values, a view that usually implies an emotional attitude. But the modern reader can understand this historical evaluation only in an intellectual sense. The chance that he can see values in Addison in just the way Pope, Steele, Gay, Swift or another contemporary did is completely remote. Feeling values and understanding that another feels values are two different things. In reading literature the first leads to a living poem, the second to a fossil. What the annotator is really doing, though unwittingly, is attempting to do the work of the poet. The poet is the only one who can indicate his attitude toward Atticus, and the poem is the only legitimate place to look for that indication.

There are no "facts" in the character of Atticus either to explain or justify. The poet has no intention of conveying fact. He shows us values and attitudes. There is no question of historical validity in the character of Atticus because such an ideal is irrelevant to the poet's aim. Even if the poet were attempting to draw a valid portrait of Joseph Addison, he would never use the satiric mode, for in this mode he and his audience agree that what he has written is not "true," but a distortion. Alexander Pope saw Joseph Addison as a symbol of certain values; at least at one time he did. It is hard to believe that Pope ever wondered whether what he had written was "true" or not. He would have recognized that such a question is not to be asked. Atticus lives in the poem, but not out of it.

The second assumption of the annotators is that their details are meaningful and complete. The Atticus lines usually inspire only an account of Pope's relationship to Addison and a history of the publication of the lines. But if all this is significant, an important question should be asked. Why should Pope reproduce these lines some twenty years later? Surely he is not, as the implication seems to be, pursuing Addison well beyond the grave.[7] The lines have long since served any propagandistic function they might originally have had. They had been published, so pride in composition would seem to be a vanity which, if it existed, had already been satisfied. On the face of it, Pope's quarrel with Addison is utterly inadequate to motivate the lines in the poem. But this is not a point most annotators make.

Also left unexamined is the fact that the lines on Atticus outside the poem make a different point from the lines placed in the context of the *Epistle to Dr. Arbuthnot*. By themselves the lines are an attack on a formidable opponent. The impression is that Atticus, who is compared to the Turk and to Cato, is a man of significance whose actions are of some consequence. Such a tyrant of genius and fame is to be reckoned with. But Atticus of the epistle is a man of wasted genius. The contrast with the poet shows him to be a man whose moral failings have condemned him to a narrow circle and negligible influence. He is not a figure to be feared, and the line "Who would not weep if Atticus were he?" takes on a deeper poignance and pathos in the epistle. But the usual account of Pope and Addison leaves the impression that the purpose of the lines in the epistle is the same as the purpose of the original lines on Atticus.

There remains unexamined also the question of why Pope should revive an attack after so long a time. A very satisfactory answer to this is that Pope is not reviving his quarrel. Certainly he no longer saw Addison as an opponent or enemy. The obvious answer is that from a perspective of many years he saw in this experience values that transcended his own resentment and anger. These are the values he gives the lines in the poem. In some ways they are alike, but they are also significantly unlike the values he emphasized in the heat of the literary argument. The values he saw in his experience he worked into the Epistle. As modern readers we would be wise to look for the poet's meaning where it is stated unequivocally, in the *Epistle to Dr. Arbuthnot*.

Though Pope's poem reveals little as biography, as belief it throws light upon the whole age. It is not an argument, not even a defense really. It is a credo passionately stated. We often hear that for Pope art was a vehicle for conveying moral instruction. It sounds mechanical and coldly intellectual. The *Epistle to Dr. Arbuthnot* shows how sadly inadequate such a statement is. Here is the burning belief that great art is created out of the moral urge, that immorality leads to bad art. Here there is no question of conveying; there is only the question of being. The great poet wants above all to be known as a good man. Only through that ideal, not through a selfish desire for fame, can he achieve greatness.

There is a good deal of truth to the assertion that Pope's poem has persuasive rhetoric in it, but it does not do the poem full justice to interpret it as a speech. The poet and the orator might both be called moving speakers, but the similarity is at least partly semantic. The orator directs his words to an audience. He finds his listeners in a certain mood with a given set of convictions. His task is to understand their moods or their minds—more likely both—and reinforce or change them. His purpose is conviction. That is his excuse for being. The poet may also speak for conviction, but he does not plead; he asserts. The epistle, though addressed to one man and intended ultimately for many readers was written for the poet. Like most great satiric and non-satiric art it was written for the believer, not the skeptic. It is a statement of values, the credo of a poet.

Satiric Ambiguity

POPE'S *Epistle to Dr. Arbuthnot* ILLUSTRATES NEATLY THE FREEdom any artist feels in using both satiric and non-satiric technique in the same work. The poem develops by contrasts and in the end states its point more positively than ironically. The contrasts are absolute, and in this respect the *Epistle to Dr. Arbuthnot* is like most satire. But a good deal of the best satiric writing is not so straightforward. The spectacular reclassification of the Houhyhnhmns from "ideal" to "comic" furnishes proof that even the perfection of nature may be called in question, and Parson Adams, Sir Roger de Coverley, and Walter Shandy—three of the most delightful characters of any period—have never suffered from the critic's inability to give them labels.

Ambiguity in satire springs from a weakening of one of the satiric traits. The first source may be an inconclusive disapproval of the satirized object. Sir Roger's faults, for example, are nicely balanced by his virtues. Whether the Houyhnhmns are ideal or comic—or both—is more a matter of interpretation, but ambiguous for the same reason. The essay entitled "*The Vicar of Wakefield* and the Kindly Satirist" tries to show just where satiric ambiguity of this sort exists in Goldsmith's novel and how it contributes to the effectiveness of both character and plot.

The second source of satiric ambiguity is a weakening of the ironic agreement between author and audience. Johnson's *Rasselas* serves as a good example here because its moral tone might seem at first glance to promise a serious, non-satiric presentation, though closer examination shows that some of Rasselas' adventures are satiric, some are obviously not, while a third group cannot be classified with certainty. This variety and ambiguity reinforce the ironic nature of the plot.

The ambiguity of *Rasselas* is possible and desirable because of its plot, which is of special significance in any discussion of Johnson's narrative. The essay on *Rasselas*, then, begins with a detailed discussion of its plot and with general comment on the ironic, nonchronological qualities that so often characterize satiric plot.

The Vicar of Wakefield and the Kindly Satirist

So long as satire is defined in terms of subject matter or purpose, the satirist seems to remain essentially a man of moral indignation whose honest purpose is reform of his society, and, of course, the popular image of the satirist as propagandist is a conception the writers themselves have often insisted upon. If he is no longer required to demonstrate a passion for reforming the world, the harsh front of the moralist may fade and reveal the patient, humorous, ironic smile of the kindly satirist. He has other masks, of course, but the sympathetic satirizing of the naive character has been so successful that a discussion of satiric technique would be incomplete without it.

Naïveté is a quality that encourages ambivalence. The honest, upright man who passes through the temptations and vicissitudes of life with a pure and unsullied soul is a character to be envied and admired. His childlike innocence, his trust, his spotless life, and his unshaken faith are virtues attainable by few men. In all honesty, however, it must be said that not many men really want such virtues. It is small comfort to win the game if one doesn't know the score. Such simple triumphant characters inspire respect, but condescension, too.

The Vicar of Wakefield is just such a character. He is especially interesting, for Goldsmith used the technique of the more severe satirists, but with a more complex attitude. He has a different purpose, a different object, and achieves, finally, a different result. First he makes ambiguous the degree to which the Vicar is satirized. Innocence and optimism are good, but the reader of normal sensitivities soon sets a point at which virtue and foolishness seem to blend. Then, too, to complicate the simple parson even more, Goldsmith shifts his satiric object during the course of the book. Of course, the reader must grasp all this without help from the Vicar, for that good man cannot moralize his own fable.

It is important, though perhaps no longer necessary, to say that the *Vicar of Wakefield* is not a sentimental novel. In an article published in 1933, W. F. Gallaway[1] argued that the connections of Goldsmith's book with the sentimental novel are not so direct nor so simple as might immediately seem to be the case. He held that in the Vicar, Goldsmith "set out to describe a gullible sentimentalist." For the novel itself, "Goldsmith was, so it seems, writing to counteract the effects of sentimental novels."

Whether or not these were Goldsmith's actual purposes, the *Vicar of Wakefield* does not offer the reader a sentimental world view. Though Parson Primrose sees the world in simple terms, the vision of the satirist records the same world in ambivalences. A sentimental author would not agree with Goldsmith, for it is characteristic of sentimentalism that it does not allow an ambivalent attitude toward its ideals. The sentimentalist creates a world around him consistent with his own values and then lives in it. Happiness becomes a personal rather than a social state. A man who acts in this way, whether he be Yorick or Richard II, will seem to act without restraint and to indulge in emotion "for its own sake." Actually such descriptions, though common enough as definitions of sentimentalism, attempt to analyze the sentimentalist from the point of view of "the real world." Judging the sentimentalist by his own assumptions, his actions are as understandable and as predictable as anyone else's. The realist, who is an empiricist, does not regard the conversion of a hardened criminal as credible, for such things seldom happen in actual experience. The sentimentalist, who judges by principle, would regard such an event as eminently believable if it were consistent with his created world.

This description of the sentimentalist might make it seem that though Goldsmith is not sentimental, the Vicar himself is. Gallaway, just quoted above, is an example of a critic who thinks so. "It seems that Goldsmith set out to describe the disasters of the gullible sentimentalist, as he knew them from observation and experience, but was prevented by a growing love for his own creation from leading him beyond the brink of what in any existing society would have been inevitable ruin." Similarly, he remarks that Dr. Primrose "himself is a victim of his own virtue, a thorough sentimentalist in his trust of man and in his contentment with the simple life at Wakefield." It is certainly true that the Vicar often acts like a sentimentalist, but a similarity of action by no means implies that he acts from sentimental motives.

Although the Vicar is in many ways a simple man, he is not easily categorized. There is first of all the difference in mood and tone between the first and second halves of the book[2] and second the fact that Goldsmith's satiric object shifts as the mood changes. The third complication is that though the reader may disapprove, he is still sympathetic.

Through the first sixteen chapters the Primroses live in innocent and happy circumstances. Barring the rather vague catastrophe that forces them to leave Wakefield, the life which the Vicar describes is uneventful and innocent. The family itself is "generous, credulous, simple, and inoffensive." Surely this is a delightful scene. But the Vicar can describe it as he does only because he does not recognize the potential for evil that the situation holds. The reader knows; he suspects Ned Thornhill's intentions immediately.

But it is not the Vicar's assumptions that keep him from seeing the truth, for within his own family circle he is wise, even sly. Though he does not recognize Lady Blarney and Miss Skeggs for what they are, he comments on them with penetration: "Their finery, however, threw a veil over any grossness in their conversation."[3] (Chap. IX) Later, as he returns with the worthless draft, he remarks that his wife and daughters "bore my disappointment with great resignation, as it was eclipsed in the greatness of their own." (Chap. XIV) Some of his remarks might have come from *Rasselas:* "Conscience is a coward; and those faults it has not strength enough to prevent, it seldom has justice enough to accuse." (Chap. XIII)

Although the Vicar is wise in his family, he is unable to judge the motives of men in the outside world. He does not think everyone at the fair is honest; he simply does not know how to identify those that are not. He remarks at various times on the evil qualities of Ned Thornhill, Mr. Burchell, Mr. Wilmot, Ephraim Jenkinson, and others. He does not believe that all men are good, though the fact that he accepts men for what they are, or what they seem to be, gives much the same impression. Outside his own family, he is a man unable to identify, much less unveil, hypocrisy. A sentimentalist would mistake the Squire because he thought all men good or because he instinctively trusted him. The Vicar does neither. He makes an error in judgment. He is a victim of his lack of knowledge of men, not of his own virtue. His virtue is his saving quality. The reader who does not make a distinction at this point between virtue and bad judgment loses Goldsmith's creation of a man who lives in a world in which appearances are real. Until adversity falls upon him, the Vicar is far from being a sentimentalist. Judging as he does from observation, the Vicar, in spite of the critics, can only be called an empiricist. In fact, his difficulty arises because his empiricism is absolute—without theory, conjecture, or practical reservation.

The narrative development of the *Vicar of Wakefield* grows out of this trait of naïveté, especially as it appears in the Vicar himself.

Contrary to one rather general impression, the plot has a clear coherent development. Three critical, well motivated actions lead to the crisis of the Vicar's imprisonment. The first comes when Olivia elopes with the Squire (Chapter XVII). The second is the Vicar's signing the bond in order to obtain George's commission (Chapter XXI). The last event leading to the impasse of the second half is the Vicar's refusal to sanction the wedding of the Squire and Miss Wilmot (Chapter XXIV). George's challenge (Chapter XXVIII) is a part of the same pattern, but it does not have a significant effect upon the development of the action.

Olivia's elopement and the Vicar's bond are attributable to naive misjudgment based upon a lack of knowledge of men, and it is this characteristic which Goldsmith is satirizing. Indeed, a good part of the eight chapters preceding Olivia's flight is devoted to emphasizing this characteristic in the Vicar. Lady Blarney and Miss Skeggs and the argument over Mr. Burchell's letterbook (Chapters IX–XV) and the developments in the elopement plot bring out the Vicar's lack of knowledge of women and men. The sale of the colt certainly shows a gullible man, indeed little more. This same lack of knowledge is shown in the Vicar's belief of the Squire's story (Chapter XVIII), his entertainment by the butler (Chapter XIX), and his signing of the bond to assure George's commission (Chapter XXI). These are the actions of a man with poor judgment. Although they have been motivated, the reader is constantly aware that the actions are foolish, and he accepts the narrator's evaluation with conscious irony.

The second half of the book, beginning with the discovery of Olivia in Chapter XXI, shows the Vicar in adversity. The seduction of Olivia introduces sorrow, crisis, and anxiety where before there had been good humor, kindly concern, and an expectation of happiness. And the Vicar's refusal to abandon Olivia's claim on the Squire, first stated in Chapter XXIV, is a different sort of crisis. It develops out of knowledge rather than innocence, for the Vicar has changed. He has learned how mistaken his judgment has been; he is no longer naive, at least so far as Squire Thornhill is concerned. Goldsmith's satire now takes a different object—long-suffering, hopeful Christian optimism. The Vicar, who had judged solely by appearances, now makes decisions by principle alone, a kind of sentimentalism by definition though not, except in the conversion of the prisoners, the conventional literary sort. The great mass of evidence that Providence favors the wicked and oppresses the innocent only confirms his belief in the justice of God. He has abandoned his empiricism for the principles of Christianity. The satire at this point is ambiguous, for the author cannot nudge the reader perceptibly. Each reader can argue the degree though he cannot bring Goldsmith to testify.

The Vicar's new sophistication makes the old object of satire unsuitable, and the state of the plot makes the new one, Christian optimism, likely. The plot at this point is at an impasse. The main character refuses to act, and he can hardly be reduced to lower circumstances. The narrative cannot develop, so Goldsmith substitutes for it the incremental repetition characteristic of so much satiric narrative. He uses a pattern of similar actions building to an emotional climax. The series of blows ending in George's arrest and certain fate are climaxed by the Vicar's sermon, an emotional as well as theological statement expressing the basis of his actions in the second part of the novel. After the sermon, the narrative resumes, and the plot is resolved.

But Goldsmith's satire on Christian optimism is not simple, for in addition to the ambiguity of the attack, there is a constant note of ambivalence. The reader first meets the Vicar's new attitude at the time of the arrest in Chapter XXV. Though the Vicar expounds sound doctrine, he seems to protest too much.

> "What! my friends," cried I, "and is this the way you love me? Is this the manner you obey the instructions I have given you from the pulpit? Thus to fly in the face of justice, and bring down ruin on yourselves and me? Where is your ringleader? Show me the man that has thus seduced you. As sure as he lives he shall feel my resentment. Alas! my dear deluded flock, return back to the duty you owe to God, to your country and to me."

The sermon in Chapter XXIX on the equal dealings of Providence provides the climax of the Vicar's optimism. It is also a masterful example of satiric ambivalence. The Vicar preaches good doctrine, but the sympathetic reader is not likely to be quite so resigned as the Vicar. He is also familiar enough with literary conventions to know that the Vicar will not have to wait until eternity for his happiness. He will get it in a chapter or so.

The Vicar is something of a parallel to Lemuel Gulliver. Both are naive, and both learn. Gulliver's tone and attitude shift markedly in his fourth voyage. The Vicar learns, and as he does the tone of his book shifts too, but he does not denounce as Gulliver does. Even though the Vicar understands, there is nothing he can do to escape his impasse. The difference may lie partly in the fact that Gulliver has learned a lesson; the Vicar has been taught one.

The ending of the *Vicar of Wakefield* has been called both sentimental and a parody on sentimental novels. Hilles has remarked upon its appropriateness to the plot. A further point can be made. The ending of any book is strongest when it is consonant with both plot and theme. Goldsmith's view of the Vicar has been consistently ambivalent. His naïveté is both appealing and frustrating. Also, Goldsmith has dealt with two sides of the Vicar in the two parts of the book. As far as the Vicar's naïveté is concerned, the ending confirms the author's satiric view. Virtue unprotected by a knowledge of men is Parson Primrose's motivating characteristic. Without it, the *Vicar of Wakefield* could not exist. Although the discussion of this quality has been limited to the Vicar himself, the trait motivates his whole family. Olivia, Moses, and Mrs. Primrose act upon it, and so do George and Sophia, though less spectacularly. The naïveté of the family leads it to an utterly helpless condition. Then all are rescued by the great and good Sir William Thornhill, though by means of his greatness rather than his goodness. The Primroses attract Sir William because they are virtuous, and the Squire is vulnerable because, as a kind of counterpart of the Vicar, he exhibits evil without adequate knowledge of men (Jenkinson and the butler) or the power that gives him leave to act (Sir William). But the rescue takes place primarily because Sir William wants it to. The Vicar prospers only so long as he is protected by a superior power, though such a power does not prevent natural catastrophes like the fire or moral lapses like Olivia's. Such an ending has a genuine and honest relationship to the plot. It states the only condition under which the Vicar and his family could be happy. A man who is merely moral is very foolish. He can be swindled and deceived. Such a man can hope for happiness only so long as he possesses nothing that men less moral and more sophisticated want. Surely there is a realistic ethic in operation here. The satiric view is justified.

But there is another side to the Vicar. He is a hopeful, Christian optimist, resigned even in the face of tragedy and injustice. But he makes a virtue of his helplessness, arguing in his sermon that unhappiness really makes for greater happiness. He is so insistent that he fosters the feeling that the author is giving the reader a knowing look. But the reader's practical view this time is too narrow; the Vicar is right, at least this once. Goldsmith makes the point doubly clear by making Mr. Burchell one who walks among men unrecognized and unhonored. At the right moment, he returns in all his power, rewarding the virtuous and punishing the guilty. He even comes as a bridegroom. At this point the justified satirist becomes slightly uncomfortable.

However the ending be described, it is adequate and appropriate to the plot. It also gives climactic support to Goldsmith's consistently ambivalent view of the Vicar. The Vicar's innocence is both appealing and amusing to most readers, but naïveté is not invariably attractive, only as it occurs with other qualities. The country bumpkin, for example, is not sympathetic. The Vicar, however, has a generous sprinkling of shrewd, sly wit mixed with his naïveté. His wise sentences show that he is not contemptible intellectually. Further, the Vicar is moral, though he is satirized. A lack of knowledge of men prompts him to act foolishly, and the amusement and laughter his misjudgments arouse are clear evidence of the author's and the reader's disapproval.

But sympathetic disapproval is a paradox that asks for elucidation. What is there in Goldsmith's treatment that leads to kindly satire? Since satiric treatment rests upon three distinctive traits, some answer might come from watching all three work in the character and values of the Vicar: a contrast in values, an unfavorable attitude in the reader, and an ironic agreement between author and reader as to the truth and validity of the presentation.

The Vicar's lack of knowledge of men is the trait under satiric treatment, and the contrasting value is both implied in the action and exemplified in such diverse characters as Sir William Thornhill and Ephraim Jenkinson. The reader is obviously led to disapprove, though he is sympathetic. But this is too simple an explanation, for the same can be said of Achitophel, whom Dryden praises, and of Atticus, for whom the reader must weep. If the case of the Vicar is typical, the kindly satirist makes the virtues of his object moral ones, at the same time making his faults something amoral such as mistaken judgment. The Vicar and a character like Achitophel are not regarded in the same way. Dryden's character is a serious, threatening personality, so much so that the irony of the reader's acceptance is not something of which he is always conscious. The Vicar may cause difficulty to his friends and family, but he is not a threat to his society.

Since the Vicar's moral virtues extenuate his error, the reader's disapproval is weakened. Rather than moral denunciation, he tends to show condescension, pity, or even compassion. In addition, the reader's own sophistication makes him constantly aware that his acceptance of the Vicar's world is ironic. Goldsmith makes the reader, and the reader alone, omniscient, and to know all is to forgive the Vicar.

The Plot of *Rasselas*

Plot or plan is almost always looked upon as a weak point in satiric works. *Hudibras* is unfinished. *Absalom and Achitophel* concludes before the action is completed. The *Rape of the Lock* does not resolve any disagreement. *Gulliver's Travels* is episodic with the third voyage much like an interpolation. *Rasselas* was never completed. Such startling failure among a group of masterpieces does, however, arouse suspicion that the "failures" may be due to lack of discernment in the critic, as recent criticism suggests, rather than deficient structure in the work of art.

The modern concept of plot and development centers primarily on character. The debate over the status of *Moll Flanders* as a novel, for example, often turns upon the question of whether the character of Moll develops during the course of the book. If it does, one argument runs, the book is a novel. There is a further assumption among most readers that the characters should act in an understandable way. Such an understanding makes the plot seem inevitable. Perhaps a reader cannot predict what a character will do in any particular situation, but at the end of the novel he can look back and see that from an Olympian point of view the action was predictable. It is characteristic of a good deal of successful fiction that it makes alternative decisions seem possible during the action, but at the end—sometimes during the course of the plot— the reader sees that most of these decisions were not made among genuine alternatives, for the character was actually capable of only one course. The action in retrospect seems inevitable.

Most plots show two kinds of inevitability—time and action. The early history of fiction shows respect for time, but the action according to modern standards, is episodic or inadequately motivated. The convention that time is inevitable was disregarded first by Sterne, then notably by Joyce, and now by numerous writers. But Sterne and Joyce were forced into an inevitability of character —or the mind—that was absolute.

Shakespeare is the great exponent of the inevitability of time and action. Perhaps this is his most pervasive influence on English and American literature. With Shakespeare the motivation of a character is tangible. Action is seen; statements are heard. This is the nature of the dramatic as he practiced it, and it is a fundamental technique of presentation in a great deal of fiction. With

Sterne the unity is not seen so tangibly. It lies outside the action in the mind of the main character or narrator. It can be inferred, but hardly examined. The technique of Shakespeare does not require, though it undoubtedly encourages, the artist to include some point in his work at which the reader can look back and either see or review the course of the characters of the drama or novel. Most artists regard inevitable action as meaningful as it leads to decisions and consequences of great significance. An important action of some finality is almost an artistic necessity. A very careful building of character is necessary to show the inevitable action.

The technique of Sterne does not require the final important action with its attendant sophisticated view of previous incidents. In the drama the convention of the climax for a long time seemed almost unbreakable, though *Waiting for Godot* showed how if the convention of cause and effect were rejected the climax became unnecessary too. If *Hamlet* were to close with Act III it would be unfinished. But *Tristram Shandy* is not unfinished in the same sense because a final resolution is not a necessary part of the convention with which the author is working.

Satiric narrative, though it superficially resembles the fiction of the late seventeenth and early eighteenth centuries, is really a compromise between the Shakespearean and Shandean techniques. Time as a convention is accepted without any apparent question, though the chronological relationship of events is often not significant. The unity lies in the mind of the narrator or in the theme rather than in a cause and effect relation. It is not a valid criticism of *Gulliver's Travels* to say that a particular chapter could be omitted without affecting the action of the book in any way, for the technique of the author does not everywhere depend on a cause and effect relationship.

When inevitable action tends toward some final climactic event, the reader's recognition of the ultimate significance of such action is delayed until the end. The actions of Lear can be seen in their true proportions only after the death of Cordelia. Though the actions of Gulliver gain from being considered in toto, the reader does understand their true significance throughout. There is no absolute necessity for a final action. Something like a climax may be obtained from presenting values in an ascending order of seriousness, leading to increased emotion on the part of the reader. As the values become more significant the action seems to develop.

But this kind of change is different in kind from dramatic development. It is the end of a series of insights rather than the key insight.

The notions of connection and completion lie in the author and reader, not in the actions themselves. Both are necessary for the further notion of climax. The satirist is not bound to the conventions of either completion or climax, yet they are so ingrained in author and reader that he often makes a gesture toward both.

The great Augustan satires were written when interest in detailed character portrayal or development was relatively slight, even in the drama. The compromise between the Shakespearean and Shandean techniques meant that the satirists did not have to develop character for their art. Besides, satire seems to discourage detailed development of character, since details tend to blur the character as a representative. This discouragement is not inevitable. Achitophel is a complex character, though it is not Dryden's purpose to put him into a variety of situations. Conventions change. Representative characters like Moll, Robinson Crusoe, and Pamela seem pale chiefly because of the demand we make on our own writers for rich and full detail.

When an author has the portrayal of character as his concern, incident tends to have an inherent value. In simple plot fiction the incident has the same value. In satiric fiction the action may be interesting or amusing for itself, but it also has a direct and immediately recognizable part in the author's satiric purpose. It is in some way symbolic and obviously so. Of course symbolic incident occurs in other kinds of fiction, but recognition of its immediate significance gives a work like *Rasselas* a simple-seeming exterior that belies its profoundly moving theme.

The plot of *Rasselas* has all the "faults" usually found in a satiric work. It is episodic, digressive, and incomplete. It is such a typical example of what critics attack in satire, that even though perceptive work has been done on it in recent years, it makes a useful illustration of the symbolic nature of satiric plot.[1]

The attack on this element of Johnson's work is of long standing and has the support of eminent critics. It has not prevented universal approbation of the tale itself, only tempered it somewhat.

> *Rasselas* does not so much end as break off. His contemporaries supposed that Johnson intended to write a continuation, but it seems equally likely that once he had written enough to fill the two small volumes he had agreed to deliver, he

stopped because he did not like to write and because, in this particular case, he did not know what more to say.[2]

Before beginning with the plot itself, it will be well to say that with *Rasselas* we are not dealing with a satirized character. He knows that he is ignorant in that he has not found a *choice of life,* and he is naive in thinking that he can make the choice he hopes to, but Johnson does not express any disapprobation of Rasselas for either quality. Candide and Rasselas are so often mentioned together that we might well conclude there is some basic similarity in this regard.[3] Both are naive, of course, and both are travelers among Satiricans, but Candide's naïveté is a constant subject of satire. He is a naive actor in a sentimental farce. Rasselas is not; he is a seeker. Johnson's own phrase *Choice of life* actually does not do justice to what it is that Rasselas is seeking. What Rasselas really feels is a restlessness, a dissatisfaction. Though he has all that the world can offer, the world cannot satisfy him. This is no mere desire to know what to do in life. This is nothing more nor less than the great Faustian dissatisfaction with everything that life can give. In theme and purpose, though not throughout in technique, there is a more meaningful comparison to be made with *Faust* than with *Candide.* Rasselas is not a titan, for Johnson did not believe in titans. He is more like a fairly rational Everyman, searching for some course of life that will lead to human happiness.

Johnson thinks in terms of general truth, and Rasselas as a representative of the human race is consistent with his thinking. The description of the Happy Valley is a representation of the world that God gave man. On this earth there is every reason to think he could be happy. The difficulty with Rasselas, and with man, is that Paradise is not enough. The explanation lies in what Rasselas says to the animals: "nor do I, ye gentle beings, envy your felicity, for it is not the felicity of man." This is the great principle of decorum. Everything acts according to the laws of its nature, and man is no exception. But the nature of man is unique. Man is the result of special creation, and by that special creation he is forever differentiated from anything else on earth. As Rasselas says, and his actions prove it, "Man has surely some latent sense for which this place affords no gratification, or he has some desires distinct from sense, which must be satisfied before he can be happy." Not only is he discontented, he does not understand the cause of his discontent.

'That I want nothing,' said the prince, 'or that I know not

95

what I want, is the cause of my complaint; if I had any
known want, I should have a certain wish; that wish would
excite endeavour, and I should not then repine to see the sun
move so slowly towards the western mountain. . . . I have
already enjoyed too much; give me something to desire.[4]

Though the character Rasselas is generalized and bloodless, his
situation is one to which every reader can respond sympathetically.
His ignorance and discontent arise not from misjudgment but from
the human condition.

The plot and most of the incidents of *Rasselas* are symbols of
ironic failure, and even before the prince leaves the Happy Valley,
we are shown in his aviator friend a prototype of the events which
are to follow. Suspense is built up for a flying escape; and the in-
ventor even delivers a speech filled with sensible maxims and
ideas.

'If men were all virtuous,' returned the artist, 'I should with
great alacrity teach them to fly. But what would be the security of the good, if the bad could at pleasure invade them
from the sky? Against an army sailing throught the clouds,
neither walls, nor mountains, nor seas, could afford any
security.'[5]

After a year of work, he stands on a little promontory, waves his
pinions in the air, and falls into the lake. Johnson adds, "His
wings, which were of no use in the air, sustained him in the
water. . . ." This is the pattern Rasselas is to meet on the outside:
the ironic failure. It seems at first that each person Rasselas meets
has something important to offer him, and often the person himself
thinks so, or pretends at least. But time after time the climax is
ironic, and this irony is the basic element of the plot.

The greatest and most pessimistic irony of all is that apparently
there is no answer to Rasselas's question or his discontent. There
is no choice of life. But as Johnson presents it, this conclusion is not
shattering; rather it produces something like pathetic irony. The
characters are helpless, and accept their lot with resignation.

This ironic search for what does not exist is repeated in the book
in three different patterns. Most comprehensive is Rasselas' search
for something that will bring happiness or satisfy the restlessness
he feels. This is the overall pattern. The second is the history of
Imlac. Third are the individual adventures or incidents in which
Rasselas, Nekayah, Imlac, and Pekuah are engaged first together,
then separately, then together again. Each of these incidents, though

a unit in itself, repeats and contributes to the greater pattern. An examination of the incidents shows that they are not mere repetition. Each has something of its own to contribute.

The history of Imlac is a very fine artistic bit, pointing up one of the basic themes, the irony of the search itself. Here at the outset is provided for Rasselas the answer, or rather the lack of answer, that he is looking for. Imlac has been through the same thing that Rasselas is to go through. He has failed in his search, just as Rasselas is going to fail. But all this makes no difference to Rasselas. He cannot learn from the experience of others, only from his own. By placing Imlac's history at the beginning, even before Rasselas' escape from the Happy Valley, Johnson is emphasizing one of the pathetic, tragic ironies of human existence, that each generation must learn for itself. Realization of this fundamental irony is the only thing that allows the ending to function as a conclusion. It is indeed a conclusion in which nothing is concluded, as the title of Chapter XLIX proclaims, but it is the end of Rasselas's book just as the end of Imlac's history is the end of Imlac's book. It is the conclusion of a cycle, a cycle that must be repeated for each man and for each generation. Each man's history will vary in details, just as Imlac's history takes a different development and at times shows a different apparent purpose from that of Rasselas. But all will follow the same pattern, an observation quite in keeping with the philosophic nature of Johnson's mind.

Imlac's history is not so obviously a search for happiness as that of Rasselas is, but the same can be said for the lives of most men. We see in Imlac the same pattern: the rejection of happiness as expounded to him by his parent; his search for it, with particular reference to knowledge; his eventual failure to find it; and finally his refuge in the Happy Valley, where he has at least the consolation of knowledge though he does not have happiness. Imlac gives Rasselas good advice;

'Sir,' answered the poet, 'your escape will be difficult, and, perhaps, you may soon repent your curiosity. The world which you figure to yourself smooth and quiet as the lake in the valley, you will find a sea foaming with tempests, and boiling with whirlpools: you will be sometimes overwhelmed by the waves of violence, and sometimes dashed against the rocks of treachery. Amidst wrongs and frauds, competitions and anxieties, you will wish a thousand times for these seats of quiet, and willingly quit hope to be free from fear.'[6]

97

But this discussion is of no effect, for Rasselas must learn for himself.

On a literal level Rasselas is alive at the beginning and the end. His active search begins, however, with a symbol of birth and ends in the tomb. In Chapters XIII and XIV, Rasselas leaves the shelter and protection of the Happy Valley, and after great labor—Johnson's word—is born into the world. Rasselas and his friends then begin their active observation of the world in Chapter XVII.

The first unit of the search includes Chapters XVII–XXII. Rasselas searches alone in the first two incidents (XVII–XVIII), Imlac and Nekayah join him for the third, fourth, and fifth (XIX–XXI), and Rasselas is again alone in the sixth (XXII). This unit is based upon the ironic expectation that happiness can be found according to certain principles or amid certain physical surroundings. Lives of gratification, patience, pastoral simplicity, prosperity, solitude, and obedience to natural law are all examined and found wanting.

From the first experiences, Rasselas learns that his search is more difficult than he had expected. He therefore decides to divide the search with his sister and to ask the question more humbly. Rasselas looks at the courts, Nekayah toward the shades of domestic life to see whether happiness can be found (Chapters XXIII–XXIX). The structure of this section is like a duet. Rasselas finds hatred in high station (XXIV); Nekayah finds the daughters idle and vain (XXV). Nekayah describes the families to Rasselas (XXVI); Rasselas describes high place to Nekayah (XXVII). This section concludes with a debate on marriage by both the prince and princess (XXVIII–XXIX).

The third section (Chapters XXX–XXXIX) deals with a corollary of the search, not what leads to happiness, but what causes unhappiness. Several answers are offered. Pekuah, afraid of the dead that cannot harm her, returns to apparent safety, where she is kidnapped (XXXIII). Nekayah then enters into a ritual of grief (XXXIV–XXXVI), and by an act of will keeps her unhappiness alive, though Pekuah is actually safe. Pekuah relates her adventures while being held by the Arab who kidnapped her (XXXVIII–XXXIX), and here the attention should be centered on the Arab rather than on Pekuah. He too is making his own evil. After a struggle, he rejects the intellectual companionship of Pekuah, who could make life less tedious for him. He takes gold instead, though the gold can only bring him more possessions, which he already knows do not bring happiness, or allow him to increase the size of his seraglio, which is also not a source of happiness. He accepts as valuable the thing the world regards as valuable, though obviously it has not brought him happiness.

This section, dealing as it does with man's compulsion to create his own unhappiness, is a digression in subject matter and technique, though a valuable addition to Johnson's discussion of the main theme, for here we find what might be called ironic success.

The next section deals with men who, though they may not have found happiness, have come to some sort of terms with the difficulties of life and give at least an appearance of happiness (XL–XLVII). The learned astronomer offers the seekers for happiness one of the most ironic of their discoveries: This, one of the wisest of all men, is mad. His madness is intertwined with great knowledge, great integrity, and impressive maxims of morality. The astronomer is an impressive symbol of the vanity of human knowledge, but Johnson has Imlac point out particularly that happiness is not to be found in vain speculations. The astronomer's imagination predominated over his reason, and "All power of fancy over reason is a degree of insanity." Having accepted this principle from Imlac, in the very next chapter (XLV) the group meets an old man who sees things exactly as they are, and they are not willing to believe what they hear. A further irony arises as the astronomer is reintroduced (XLVI–XLVII), for one of the signs of his sanity is his conviction that he had made the wrong choice of life, and he is again thrown into doubt. These old men, as well as the brief discussion of monastic life (XLVII), show that those whose lives seem tranquil with the appearance of happiness offer no more than anyone else.

The visit to the dead in the catacombs and the discussion of the nature of the soul makes an appropriate end for the search that began with the birth symbol. It also stimulates Rasselas to see the futility of the search itself.

> 'Those that lie here stretched before us, the wise and the powerful of ancient times, warn us to remember the shortness of our present state: they were, perhaps, snatched away while they were busy, like us in the choice of life.'[7]

The last chapter, a rather obvious anticlimax, emphasizes the futility of answering Rasselas' question.

Johnson calls his last chapter "The Conclusion in which Nothing is Concluded." The title has meaningful ambiguity. It is a conclusion (end of the book), and it represents an intellectual conclusion (that the question cannot be answered). Nothing is concluded (no conventional ending for the tale), and no definitive intellectual conclusion is reached (that there is no answer). The symbolism of the plot allows us to answer even more completely than the anticlimactic close does. This is a question that can never be answered as it is asked. The dead stretched out in the catacombs asked the question. Imlac asked it. Rasselas asks it. And the generations that follow will ask it too. Merely asking for an answer is ironic, for it is apparent that people must learn for themselves. The question itself is ironic. Though there is no answer, there is a tentative conclusion, suggested by the incident of the kidnapping of Pekuah: Life must be accepted; we must take evil when it comes, and we can lighten the burden if we will not make it worse.

The plot of *Rasselas* is one more example of the satirist's dilemma as he begins to plot his work. He is not really interested in developing character. He cannot develop a naive character very much, for richness of detail would distract the reader. He is not primarily intent on developing character, for this implies a struggle and learning—conditions that destroy naïveté. So the satirist employs a character, uses him for his own ends, but makes a pretense or an effort at showing the character in a number of conventional fictional situations. The satirist who uses this sort of plot does not care about time, either. Time is essential where incidents operate by cause and effect, but this principle is not significant in a plot like that of *Rasselas*. Time, along with cause and effect, lead to inevitability, and Johnson is working with a different kind of relationship. He can turn time to his own uses. He can make a significant point by placing Imlac's history before Rasselas's search, and he can place his birth symbols at the beginning and death symbols at the end to show the extent of the search, but any of these could be omitted without harming the integrity of the book.

Here again *Faust* offers an illuminating comparison and contrast. Faust begins his search in much the same way Rasselas does, and with much the same reactions. In the scenes in which Faust rejects the adulation of the townspeople and the pleasures of Auerbach's cellar, Goethe follows the same satiric technique as Johnson. The only significant connection is a thematic one. But when Margaret is introduced we have a character whose values are not categorically disapproved, and Goethe's technique shifts from the satiric to the

100

non-satiric. At this point, character, time, connection, and climax become important. Though satiric thrusts are still made, the main thread of the work is no longer satiric.

But since Rasselas never finds values that are credible either to himself or the reader, Johnson never tries to create a climactic plot. Climax as it is most often used describes a point at which the characters of the plot or the audience—usually both—have greater knowledge of events which preceded or which they anticipate than they have had before. In the plot of *Rasselas,* some insights are more important than others, but there is no key insight. Rasselas' remark in the catacombs may have greater force than those which preceded it, but that is because Rasselas is being explicit. Since it does have force, Johnson is able to use it like a climax.

The unity of the plot of *Rasselas* does not lie within the events themselves, the kind of unity we expect from a drama. The unity of *Rasselas* lies in the relationship of the events to the author's theme. Although the incidents of the plot may be divided into structural units, their relationship within a unit is by theme and subject. In *Rasselas* we see a just disposition of the parts; it is aesthetically pleasing primarily because it gives greater force to each part of the theme as it is presented. Theme in satire cannot, of course, be proven; it can only be made convincing. Johnson marshals his incidents to give overwhelming validity to his point.

To say that no single satiric incident is essential to *Rasselas* is an irrelevant statement. The plot is successful, for both explicitly and symbolically it gives moving expression to Johnson's theme.

Rasselas has a special interest for anyone working with satiric technique, for it raises very clearly the question: When does the satirist become the sermonizer? The satirist misrepresents. He may do so either by distortion or unfair selection. But at times he may come close to literal accuracy, for without the grain of truth he cannot be successful. The special tone which *Rasselas* achieves grows out of the fact that some of Johnson's satire is close to truth; in some places the tacit agreement between author and reader is so weakened as to be questionable; and in many passages there is only straightforward moralizing. Apparently Boswell felt this ambiguity. In the *Life* under the year 1759, he remarks of *Rasselas* that "they who think justly, and feel with strong sensibility, will listen with eagerness and admiration to its truth and wisdom." One sentence shows explicitly that he accepted the work in the non-satiric mode: "The fund of thinking which this work contains is

101

such, that almost every sentence of it may furnish a subject of long meditation." But he shows that he cannot accept its conclusions for himself when he writes: "Notwithstanding my high admiration of Rasselas, I will not maintain that the "morbid melancholy" in Johnson's constitution may not, perhaps, have made life appear to him more insipid and unhappy than it generally is. . . ."

Actually, of course, literary presentation is not a continuum along which at one point truth becomes misrepresentation and beyond which distortion magnifies ad infinitum. Satire's grain of truth upsets this simple schema, allowing the most outrageous distortion to seem somehow in focus. The tacit agreement between author and reader is a further complication, for being tacit it does not allow the reader to know always just where the grain of truth ends and the misrepresentation begins. The callous, rational brutality of someone like the author of *A Modest Proposal* is aesthetically credible partly because it is relevant to human nature and partly because the extent of its relevance is left to the judgment of the reader.

Rasselas is especially prone to this ambiguity because of its subject matter. Enthusiastic moralists often paint a picture which the detached observer regards as exaggerated, though the picture is always presented as the truth, sometimes even as the "real truth." Boswell's comments suggest that he had been conditioned to sermons of this sort, though the natural truthfulness or gaiety of his disposition did break through. But his conditioning kept him from seeing that *Rasselas* is not cast in the usual moral mold. There is a good deal of wry, ironic comedy in *Rasselas*.[8] Rasselas' experience with the aviator is a prototype of his experiences outside the Happy Valley, and the man himself is a prototype of the people Rasselas is to meet. This artisan, as Johnson calls him, is essentially a comic figure. He promises much and delivers nothing. From self-importance, dignity, prestige, he has a sudden and disastrous fall. Johnson, of course, does not try to make his reader laugh, though he has drawn a close relative of the man in the top hat who slips on the banana peel. As a prototype of the situations which are to follow, the incident with the aviator contains obvious misrepresentation. The choices of life which follow do not promise such impossible achievement, nor can they all be said to fail so utterly. Johnson has only a grain of truth, and he uses it for satiric ends.

Rasselas' examination of life led according to nature, found in Chapter XXII, is a good illustration of Johnson's unequivocal satire. At first the Philosopher expounds his subject without interference from an unsympathetic author:

> 'Let us therefore, at length, cease to dispute, and learn to live; throw away the encumbrance of precepts, which they who utter them with so much pride and pomp do not understand, and carry with us this simple and intelligible maxim,—that deviation from nature is deviation from happiness.'

Almost anyone would agree with Boswell that there the reader has been furnished with a subject of long meditation. But the effect created is ironically overthrown and the whole presentation revealed as satiric when Rasselas asks for a definition of life led according to nature.

> 'To live according to nature, is to act always with due regard to the fitness arising from the relations and qualities of causes and effects; to concur with the great and unchangeable scheme of universal felicity; to co-operate with the general disposition and tendency of the present system of things.'[9]

Contrasting to this satiric presentation are Imlac's didactic periods. Though Johnson calls Imlac's dissertation on poetry in Chapter X an "enthusiastic fit," no critic seems disposed to question the description of the poet as anything but straightforward, informative discussion. Imlac is a wise man presented in the non-satiric mode.

> 'The Europeans,' answered Imlac, 'are less unhappy than we; but they are not happy. Human life is every where a state in which much is to be endured, and little to be enjoyed.'[10]

Between the two extremes are many incidents that might well be classified as ambiguous. Chapter XVIII, "The Prince Finds a Wise and Happy Man," should be placed in this group. The man who fails to follow his own advice is a standard satiric and comic figure; witness Parson Adams. Johnson's sage, who holds that man's reason can dominate his fancy, can doubtless be met by logical arguments, but to disregard his conclusions because he breaks down with grief upon the death of his daughter is to distort by unfair selection. Just how strong the misrepresentation is makes a topic for inconclusive debate. There is much to be said on both sides.

The dominating pattern of *Rasselas* is the movement from ignorance to knowledge, appearing on several levels. It can be seen in the large movement of the book from beginning to end. It appears between parts, as between Rasselas' questioning and Imlac's answer. It also furnishes the motif between and within particular chapters. This pattern is heightened by the accompanying interplay of satiric and non-satiric presentation. But neatness and simplicity disappear as knowledge undergoes a gradual, ironic transformation, and the reader is left with only the knowledge of his own ignorance. There is a conclusion, but it leads only to the revelation that there are the ignorant who wish to know, the ignorant who think they know, and finally the ignorant who have learned that there is a more important question.

> 'To me,' said the princess, 'the choice of life is become less important; I hope hereafter to think only on the choice of eternity.'[11]

The final chapter is an ironic postscript containing the same techniques that are distinctive in the first forty-eight chapters. It too shows search and conclusion, presenting the material satirically, non-satirically, and with ambiguity as it describes the choices of Rasselas and Nekayah, Imlac and the astronomer, and Pekuah.

The satiric elements of *Rasselas* contribute significantly to the final tone which it conveys. Against the darker background of stoical acceptance, Johnson can show scorn and ridicule, bitterness, or even kindly contempt. The early parts of the books show a fairly clear contrast between the satiric and non-satiric, but as the search continues these alternate more frequently and with less regularity. The theme of *Rasselas* is simple, but the execution is quietly varied and effective.

Boswell felt, with justification, that "Johnson meant, by shewing the unsatisfactory nature of things temporal, to direct the hopes of man to things eternal." The modern reader is less likely to follow such a direction, partly because of changing cultural assumptions, but partly too because the values expressed in *Rasselas* emphasize the cycles and the search rather than the hope that lies beyond. Its moral courage and ironic view of life may well have more significance and attraction now than ever before.

Satire and the Use of History

THE ARGUMENT THROUGHOUT THIS BOOK HAS BEEN THAT AL-
though historical fact may be one dimension of satires written in
the past, it is no longer of primary significance, being subordinate
to readings that have meaning for the modern reader. This contention should not, however, be interpreted to mean that history
or literary history should be ignored. Their uses, particularly in
understanding the text, are manifold—too numerous, certainly, to
illustrate adequately in a brief volume. But history can be misused
too, and scholarship gives many examples of how inaccurate historical interpretations can lead to a misunderstanding of both
meaning and technique. This final essay is intended to illustrate
one way in which historical material can be used by the critic.

Although *Gulliver's Travels* has always been tied to the politics
and institutions of Swift's time, history has been used somewhat
unevenly in explicating the work. The voyages to Lilliput and
Laputa have been extensively annotated by references to various
people and specific incidents; the voyages to Brobdingnag and the
Houyhnhmns relatively little. But historical comment has never
been accepted as a substitute for universal application.

"Gulliver's Third Voyage" is an attempt to throw historical light
upon a difficult critical problem—the place of Book III in the plan
of the *Travels*. Without making an effort to defend Swift against
the criticism so often leveled at this part, it does try to explain why
the voyage to Laputa might seem not only satisfactory to its author,
but actually pivotal in the relationship of the four voyages. If the
essay can achieve this end, it will have demonstrated how history
can lead to a fuller, more enlightened understanding of the satirist's art.

Gulliver's Third Voyage

If *Gulliver's Travels* has a structure, the third voyage is obviously in a key position, for unless it performs some function within the book, the voyage to the Houyhnhnms becomes little more than a resounding finale. Apparently it is not a difficult part to understand, at least not since Miss Nicholson's work on it.[1] Yet it still remains in its informing plan and purpose at least partly an enigma. It is the one problem of *Gulliver's Travels* that will not go away.

The logical assumption any critic ought to make is that there is unity within the voyage. A great work of art might conceivably be three-quarters genius and the rest merely flashes of excellence and bursts of petulance, but all experience is against it. Probability says first that since we have found unity in the other three voyages, we should be able to find at least an attempt at it here. The second point is that since Voyages I and II are related, III and IV might also be connected in some way. Finally, if I, II, and IV seem to fill some function in the whole structure, the third voyage very likely has its own purpose in the larger plan.

John Middleton Murry expresses the classic view of Voyage III.

> No one would deny two facts about the *Travels:* the first, that it is Book IV—the Yahoos and the Houyhnhnms—which make the book really formidable. To a lesser degree this holds of the Struldbrugs: at least they contribute to the final effect of intensity. The second undeniable fact is that Book III as a whole is definitely inferior to the others. It is diffuse; it lacks focus. Were it not that we should lose the Struldbrugs, it might have been entirely suppressed without much loss to the *Travels* as a whole . . . To explain this inferiority by the fact that Swift was largely incorporating without re-creating, old material is not an artistic defense—artistically, Book III remains a serious blemish on one of the world's great books— but an explanation of any sort is worth having.[2]

But this position has been under attack. Ricardo Quintana thinks Voyage III has strong artistic justification. Part IV begins psychologically where the second left off. "Like the scherzo in a traditional four-movement symphony, it [the third voyage] comes between the second and fourth movements to break the tension and prepare the way for a stronger climax than could otherwise be achieved."[3] Kathleen Williams finds unifying change: "So the 'Voyage to Laputa,' which opens among a people essentially frivolous in its refusal to face the facts of human existence, ends face to face with inescapable reality." She also sees a way in which it contributes to the plan of the book: "As a completion of the processes begun in Lilliput and Brobdingnag, and as a preparation for the resolution in Houyhnhnmland, the Laputan voyage performs its task adequately, though without the formal elegance and neatness of the other books."[4] Even more detailed in his explanation is John Sutherland in his article in *Studies in Philology*. He regards the voyage as a satire on natural science of the eighteenth century, culminating in the Struldbrugs—"a fitting climax to a satire on science, since science represents man's pretensions of understanding and controlling that nature of which our ephemeral lives are a part."[5] He argues further that the third voyage is artistically necessary in order to make Gulliver's immediate acceptance of the Houyhnhnms credible.

All these commentators contribute something, but the enigma remains. Doubtless the common reader will always agree with Mr. Murry. But the failure of the third voyage is not inexplicable. In the mind of its creator it had coherence and purpose. But that intent has been frustrated by the materials of the artist and by an audience fundamentally hostile to the author's ideals.

Like the first and second voyages, the third presents transformed material of Swift's own experience which was recognizable by his contemporaries. But this voyage does not set off the same reactions in modern readers which the other voyages do. We enjoy the satiric thrusts, but we find it difficult to generalize or universalize from the particular incidents. With some magnificent exceptions—the flying island and the Struldbrugs—we read on the allegorical rather than the symbolic level. We have the feeling that Swift is here concerned with matters which are typical of, and—what is more—probably unique to, his own milieu.

The scholarship which illuminates and grows out of the third book encourages, albeit unmeaningly, this concentration on particulars. Miss Nicholson's brilliant success in expounding the scientific background of the voyage is an example. She has shown that for the most part Swift simply set down experiments actually performed by members of the Royal Society. Critics now go directly from the academy in Lagado to the Royal Society without feeling that they have left *Gulliver's Travels* at all. The academy section especially is read as propaganda rather than imaginative literature, though the same observation holds true for the other parts of the voyage as well. A reader approaching the work on this level would naturally feel that it lacked coherence since he would be looking for some substantive connection.

The tendency of modern criticism of Voyage III is to find some meaningful pattern. All writers would agree that it is an injustice to Swift to read his work as mere propaganda, only in terms of its milieu. The work of art can be made to comment on its culture, but not at the expense of aesthetic values.

Freed of the Royal Society, the Drapier incident, and the other particulars of allegorical interpretation, what is the third voyage actually about? In general terms, it is an account of several different peoples, their actions, learning, and customs. Less generally, the third voyage takes up (1) the learning—mathematics and music—of the Laputans; (2) the government of the Laputans, with particulars on the relation of the governors and the governed; (3) the results of the Laputan's obsession with mathematics and astronomy; (4) the flying island; (5) in Balnibari, agriculture practiced by projectors and by an intelligent informed person, with brief mention of architecture and gardening; (6) a description of medical, chemical, and physical experiments; (7) experiments with language; (8) experiments in education; (9) political, medical, surgical, and linguistic schemes as they relate to the state; (10) philosophers old and new; (11) modern history; (12) a king's disregard for the obligations he owes to his subjects; (13) a view of a race of men who live forever. It doesn't matter particularly whether this list is excellent or even entirely adequate. Its use here is to indicate that the third voyage deals with a great deal more than it is given credit for. Of course, if the reader is looking only at details, the breadth escapes him.

But can we say just how inclusive this voyage is? Though this may seem a difficult question, it is not by any means impossible to answer. At least we know what some of Swift's contemporaries thought the categories of human knowledge were. The most accessible and pertinent of these surveys is Wotton's *Reflections Upon Ancient and Modern Learning,*[6] the basis of which is a classification of man's learning. Adapting Wotton's categories somewhat to fit *Gulliver's Travels,* we see that Swift touches on the following: moral and political knowledge, grammar, architecture, mathematics, natural philosophy, logic, instruments, chemistry, anatomy and optics, physic and surgery, and music. He does not deal with eloquence, poetry, statuary, painting, metaphysics, plants, and animals.

It is hardly to be expected that these topics would be developed either fully or equally. But this list makes plain that Swift is not limiting himself to the science of these people. He has created a society with an indicated body of knowledge almost as large as his own. Only after seeing that Swift is working with varied categories of human knowledge should it be said that science predominates.

To call the voyage an attack on the Royal Society, on science, or even on Moderns—though it is all these things—is to miss the underlying concept of this important part of the travels. The third voyage is the expression of a world view based upon the assumptions of the modern philosopher. While individual characters and incidents may be interpreted allegorically, such interpretations are incomplete, and if relied upon as a sole means of analysis make of the third book a hodgepodge meaningful only in its parts.

Underlying any world view is a series of assumptions, and these are clearly evident among the inhabitants Gulliver meets: self-sufficiency, pride and obsession (perhaps better called enthusiasm) stand out for all to see. But most of all these people seem to lack a moral sense. They do not recognize their relationship and obligation to other members of society. Their actions are not based upon any moral purpose. They have no convictions about nor philosophy to explain their own being. The Laputan sages, above all, symbolize this failure to understand the fundamental unity of one man and another.

The academy is an obvious example. On one level it does exhibit the impracticality of the virtuoso. On another level it does satirize the abuse of theoretical reason. Underlying these, however, is the more philosophically significant defect of the man who has no moral purpose. The accomplishments of the academy are either trivial or undesirable. Only by chance could they be otherwise. The rulers are another example. They—like the scientists, historians, grammarians, and the rest—fail to show such a basic moral purpose as acting for the common good. Failing to have a purpose, they fail. In Glubbdubdrib we see how historians have so distorted and transformed the past that its real lessons for man have been obscured or obliterated.

Swift's contention is a paradox. The "Practical" men espouse a philosophy whose most glaring fault is that it is impractical. In losing his sense of moral purpose, man loses his humanity and brings confusion down upon himself.

In his essay "Of Heroick Virtue," Sir William Temple[7] describes the practice among the Chinese ancients of epitomizing the memorable actions of a king's reign after his death and adding this to their collection of knowledge. After the practice was well begun, there "lived a King, who, to raise a new Period of Time from his own Name and Reign, endeavoured to abolish the Memory of all that had passed before him, and cause all Books to be burnt, except those of Physick and Agriculture."[8] This particular venture was a failure, as our knowledge of Confucius attests. But the third voyage is like what might have been had the king succeeded. There is no eloquence, poetry, painting, and statuary—fields in which the Ancients were acknowledged to excel. There is no inherited morality to act as Confucius' doctrines did. Architecture and gardening are despised. False history, false philosophy abound. If Confucius is a hero, these Modern sages are anti-heroes.

Clara Marburgh remarks upon Temple's failure to comprehend the "new science."[9] Most modern readers easily assume the same about Swift. They do this because they are "modern." Swift writes as he does for the excellent reason that he does "understand" the new science. From his own position as a Christian moralist he sees very clearly what the new science could mean to a civilization that had, whatever its shortcomings, nominally accepted the Christian ethic as the basis for human action. We misstate Swift's position and misinterpret his deepest objections unless we see that his opposition to the world view of the Modern is based fundamentally on moral grounds.

Looking at the third voyage from the author's own point of view, it is not a disconnected series of incidents. The whole is unified by the constant reiteration that lack of a moral conception of man's place in the world leads to a universe in anarchy. But seeing this unity intellectually will not change anyone's decision about the success or failure of the third voyage. If there were effective unity, it would not have to be articulated; it could be felt. Swift has been unable to persuade his readers to take his point of view. We feel no driving purpose and explain Swift's failure by calling the voyage "episodic."

But words like "episodic" and "hodgepodge" are not explanations. At best they are evaluations, at worst mere disapproving noises. It is, though, significant that these words, along with others like "disconnected" and "various objects of satire," should be applied so exclusively to the third voyage. Why is the third voyage so "disconnected" and the second so "connected"? Without in any way underestimating the tremendous advantage gained by the concept of the people of Brobdingnag, there is not much question that the second voyage has a good deal of "hodgepodge" quality objected against in the third. Gulliver moves from country to court. His adventures are unrelated incidents, any one of which could have been omitted without anyone's being the wiser. The conversations with the King represent a quite different subject from the incidents with the monkey, the frog, and the birds. There are two contradictory concepts of the people of Brobdingnag, one represented by the King and the other by the Maids of Honor. The character of Glumdalclich and the tenuous thread of narrative are hardly sufficient to provide much more than a superficial relating of the incidents.

Such a summary is patently unfair to the second voyage; its integrity is beyond dispute. It is unified by something beyond superficial narrative devices. That "something beyond" is a moral point of view consistent, for the most part, with our own. Because we accept Swift's moral assumptions, we are able to see validity in his presentation of human nature and human civilization. Swift sets forth his values in part negatively—Gulliver's actions and his account of life in England—and in part positively and ideally—the description of the King of Brobdingnag and his government. We recognize, though Swift does not always state them explicitly, the assumptions behind his presentation. We are able to conceive them, accept them (not along with the incidents but as a part of the incidents), and believe that the author entertained them too because for the most part they are our own assumptions.

The values underlying that part of the second voyage which concentrates on Gulliver are moral platitudes. Man is petty. He does not see his own weakness. The various branches of government are corrupt, having fallen away from noble ideals. Man should be guided by his reason. Man is proud and so on. The incidents involving Gulliver fit into a familiar ethical pattern, and we recognize their consistency. But the assumptions behind Chapter VII of the second voyage are not platitudes, and it is a measure of our own self-deception that we should continue to emphasize our agreements with Swift rather than recognizing how we diverge. Looked at in detail, Brobdingnag is not the sort of Utopia we would make. We might approve of the people's clear, smooth, compact style, but restricting a law to twenty-two words with commentary strictly forbidden seems to demand a compactness which most of us do not realize. The King rejects gunpowder, and a number of critics do strain at this. He states his theory of useful knowledge clearly and unmistakably, a theory which we can accept only insofar as honoring the man who makes "two blades of grass grow upon a spot of ground where only one grew before." The King's faith in his militia rather than a standing army, is another dream that has faded. But we ignore rather than object to the King's values. He is so forceful in denouncing what we also disapprove that we are willing to let his own ideal go unchallenged.

Unfortunately, failure to understand and retain the assumptions of the seventh chapter of Book II leaves a reader unprepared for the third voyage, for the positive ideals first adumbrated in that chapter provide the integrity for Part III. That we partly agree with Swift only adds to our confusion, for in the third voyage Swift begins to attack values we and our society hold self-evident. This fact is obscured for us because we agree that people obsessed with mathematics and music are proper objects of satire, as is silly scientific research. Not really understanding Swift's assumptions, we misinterpret his symbols to fit our own beliefs. We then blame Swift for not unifying our misinterpretation. The Laputans, we think, are not well developed; but then Swift could never have developed them to please us, for we do not believe that there is enough fundamental truth in his picture to make it significant. The modern university bears just as many affinities to the academy at Lagado as the Royal Society does, but we use the Royal Society of his own day because so many of them were dilettantes. We are serious scholars. We have even devised the evasion that Swift is attacking the abuse of science rather than science, in spite of the evidence of the second and fourth voyages against it.

Swift believes in the Ancient precepts of morality, as we do. Unlike our own, however, his position is anti-scientific and anti-intellectual. From *Gulliver's Travels* we must conclude that the happiness of man is the measure of all things. Man's ultimate good is the prime value. The free-ranging, undirected operation of the intellect is not.

> And, he gave it for his Opinion; that whoever could make two Ears of Corn, or two Blades of Grass to grow upon a Spot of Ground where only one grew before; would deserve better of Mankind, and do more essential Service to his Country than the whole Race of Politicians put together.
>
> The Learning of this People is very defective; consisting

only in Morality, History, Poetry, and Mathematics, wherein they must be allowed to excel. But the last of these is wholly applied to what may be useful in Life, to the Improvement of Agriculture and all mechanical Arts; so that among us it would be little esteemed.[10]

This is the position of the author of *Gulliver's Travels*. It is a logical step from his assumption that man's purpose is to live in a state of general happiness. Knowledge which is not useful but "innocent" is unimportant and irrelevant to life. Knowledge which is potentially dangerous to mankind's happiness is positive evil and should be suppressed. We don't believe this, but the author does.

When we read of the third voyage we often get the impression that the content and the aesthetic can be considered separately. But the basic offense of the third voyage is not that it doesn't make sense artistically, but that for us it doesn't make sense. The only part in which Swift manages to strike a really responsive note is in the voyage to Luggnagg. Every critic agrees that the Struldbrugs are effective. It is also true that this incident contains one of the few general moral statements of the third book. The Struldbrugs are a moral platitude with which we agree, and when we agree with Swift his satire seems to "improve" artistically. But here again Swift does not agree with us as thoroughly as we assume. We force him into our own mode of thinking, and as we do, fail to see the full significance of the Struldbrugs as a symbol. They are old age. They are death. They are a warning to man and especially to science. But they are more than that. If we see the voyage as a whole, the Laputans are the alpha and the Struldbrugs the omega. It is as if Gulliver were seeing the Laputans again, but this time with a prescient eye. The Struldbrugs show in a way that words cannot the life-in-death quality of a society that exists without purpose. The traditional Christian moralist knows that man is born to die, and that it is only through death that life can acquire final meaning. But the modern philosopher whose eye is upon the heavens or upon himself, not upon the proper end of man, succeeds in prolonging lives that are barren, wasted, and futile. The meaningless immortality of the Struldbrugs is in every way a climax to Part III, and it is the measure of our profound rejection of Swift's ideals that we are unable to see it as he does, a vision of truth.

The third voyage is unsuccessful because the assumptions which give it integrity are repugnant to almost any modern reader. The

objects of Swift's satire, though acceptable as objects, are not transformed into meaningful symbols. Where Swift's values vary from
our own, we adjust him to our own thinking as much as possible.
Where we cannot distort him we say he fails. We make excuses for
him and regret he didn't "develop his hints more fully." It is only
justice to Swift and honesty in ourselves to say that there is intent
in the third voyage, but an intent based on values we do not regard seriously. The voyage fails because although we think Swift
"right" in his moral platitudes, we consider his concept of the
scientific world view to be "wrong." Of course, from Swift's own
point of view he was "right." He saw the scientific view as dynamic, developing, and a challenge to the theological view. In this
fear he was most certainly "right." But the right and wrong have
been decided by history, not by rational argument. The voyage has
lost its fundamental meaning; indeed modern society assured that
its meaning was lost before it was ever written. Parts retain their
vitality and validity. But the voyage Swift intended is a museum
piece, not a living document.

II

The critic who is willing to accept the third voyage as a series of
unrelated incidents is relieved of the necessity of explaining its
function as a part of *Gulliver's Travels*. He need only marvel that
a great artist in his greatest work should so inexplicably fail. Anyone, however, who believes that Swift intended the same kind of
unifying purpose here that we feel in the other three parts must
accept the responsibility of justifying his interpretations in terms
of the whole book. Such a justification requires a brief though fresh
look at the fourth voyage as well as some explanation of Voyages
I and II.

Book IV is such a rich and moving creation that most critics
sooner or later come to it. Interpretations are multiple, and many
of them are sensitive and revealing. For the most part they sup-
plement one another as each man offers his admittedly incomplete
version of the truth that lives within Swift's symbols. It has been
called pessimistic, a masterpiece of misanthropy, a denunciation of
mankind, a great statement of the abuses of human reason, as well
as a simple, traditional, moral tale rather vividly dramatized by animal symbolism. In recent years the term "satiric comedy"[11] has
been applied with growing confidence. Most critics agree that the
Houyhnhnms in some way represent reason and that this quality,

116

with reservations, is fundamentally good. They also agree that the yahoos represent the passions and that these are evil. Everyone likes the yahoos. We all know how to react to them. The Houyhnhnms, on the other hand, cause some trouble. They seem to be an ideal, but not one that many readers feel a strong yearning to achieve. Gulliver's aspirations—his conversations with the two degenerate Houyhnhnms he keeps in his stable—seem amusing to some, even faintly ludicrous to others. Some scholars say that they laugh at the Houyhnhnms, but most of us seem to regard them in much the way we do some relatives: they are not exactly something we would like to be, it is true; yet we see in them so much of ourselves and our own hopes that whatever our final judgment there is a clear strain of seriousness in it.

The assumption that seems always to be made about the fourth voyage is that in it Swift moves entirely in the realms of imagination. There are analogues and possible sources, especially for the yahoos, but these sources have nothing to do with the book. No one has ever suggested that the dark-haired yahoo whose embraces Gulliver rejected really stood for Queen Anne, Sir Robert Walpole, or the Church in Ireland. The creatures Gulliver meets are allegorical vehicles which at least represent the possible depths of man's depravity if he allows his passions to hold sway or the impossible heights of reason which he can never achieve because of his dual nature. Without denying that this is in large part a valid interpretation, certainly it must be admitted that this sort of abstraction is not what the first three voyages would lead a reader to expect. One of the distinctive traits of Swift's imagination is that it creates from concrete particulars, not abstractions. This is a quality of the Lilliputians, Brobdingnaggians, and of the third voyage as well. We should reasonably expect that this quality would carry over into the last part.

The assumption apparently is that since we don't know any yahoos or Houyhnhnms, Swift didn't either, and if he did not know any, these creatures must function chiefly as allegories. But we may have been wrong; Swift may have known about some "real" yahoos. Some sort of yahoo-like creature was apparently a part of Sir William Temple's cyclical view of history. William Wotton refers to them ironically in the preface to *Reflections on Ancient and Modern Learning.*

> But what shall be said to those numerous Deluges, which no Body knows how many Ages before that of *Noah,* are said

to have carried away all Mankind, except here and there a
Couple of ignorant Salvages, who got to some high Mountain, and from thence afterwards replenish'd the Earth?[12]

Wotton's statement is remarkably close to the tradition mentioned
by the Houyhnhnms at the debate in the grand assembly.

He took Notice of a general Tradition, that Yahoos had not
been always in their Country: But, that many Ages ago, two
of these Brutes appeared together upon a Mountain; whether
produced by the Heat of the Sun upon corrupted Mud and
Slime, or from the Oooze and Froth of the Sea was never
known.[13]

The association of these two quotations suggests a different view
of the yahoos from that usually held. They may be, as Gulliver's
master affirms, degenerate compared to the civilization their two
progenitors survived, but they may at the same time represent mankind in the original savage state, the beginning of a new civilization. Interpreted thus, they are not abstractions, mere allegorical
figures, nor even a threat which Swift holds up before us. They are
the beginning of our own culture. Gulliver's recognition of yahoo
traits within himself is his recognition of his kinship with these
remote ancestors. His hatred of them is a measure of the distance
mankind has traversed. If we accept the yahoos as progenitors of
mankind, they have a complexity they do not have as mere allegories. Gulliver's kinship to them is a shame and a glory. He is not,
as he insists, a yahoo himself. Rather he is, as the sorrel nag calls
him, a "gentle yahoo"—noble, wellborn, removed by years of history and progress from the savage creatures whom he abhors.

Accepting the yahoos as Gulliver's most remote ancestors implies an acceptance of the cyclical theory of history. Since Swift
would have learned this sort of history from Temple, the works
of his early patron might furnish a clue to the "historical Houyhnhnms." The yahoos exist in the depths of the prehistoric past; it
might be well to search almost as far back for the Houyhnhnms.
Temple points out that the Moderns seek the Ancients as guides.
But the Ancients were not the beginning, and it is necessary "to
consider at what Sources our Ancients drew their Water, and with
what unwearied Pains."[14] "As there were Guides to those we call
Ancients, so there were others that were Guides to them, in whose
Search they travelled far and laboured long." These Ancients to
the Ancients are identified by Temple: "For whoever observes the

Account already given of the Ancient *Indian* and *Chinese* Learning and Opinions, will easily find among them the Seeds of all these *Grecian* Productions and Institutions."[15] The great respect Temple held for these moralists and philosophers can be judged from this conclusion:

> By all this may be determined, whether our Moderns or our Ancients may have had the greater and the better Guides, and which of them have taken the greater Pains, and with the more Application in the Pursuit of Knowledge. And, I think, it is enough to shew, that the Advantages we have, from those we call the Ancients, may not be greater, than what they had from those that were so to them.[16]

Temple calls the writings of Confucius "the only Remainders of the Ancient Chinese Learning."

> The chief Principle he seems to lay down for a Foundation, and builds upon, is That every Man ought to study and endeavour the improving and perfecting of his own Natural Reason to the greatest Height he is capable, so as he may never (or as seldom as can be) err and swerve from the Law of Nature, in the Course and Conduct of his Life: That this, being not to be done without much Thought, Inquiry, and Diligence, makes Study and Philosophy necessary; which teaches Men what is Good and what is Bad, either in his own Nature or for theirs; and consequently what is to be done and what is to be avoided, by every Man in his several Station or Capacity. That in this Perfection of Natural Reason consists the Perfection of Body and Mind, and the utmost or supreme Happiness of Mankind. That the Means and Rules, to attain this Perfection, are chiefly not to will or desire any Thing but what is consonant to his Natural Reason, nor any Thing that is not agreeable to the Good and Happiness of other Men as well as our own. To this End is prescribed the constant Course and Practice of the several Virtues, known and agreed so generally in the World; among which, Courtesy or Civility and Gratitude are Cardinal with them. In short, the whole Scope of all *Confutius* has writ seems aimed only at teaching Men to live well, and to govern well; how Parents, Masters, and Magistrates should rule, and how Children, Servants, and Subjects should obey.[17]

This perfection of the natural reason was not exclusively Chinese, but had also been discovered by another Ancient, the original and great hero of the kingdom of Peru, Mango Copac. He and his sister

> told the People who came first about them, that they were the Son and Daughter of the *Sun,* and that their Father, taking Pity of the miserable Condition of Mankind, had sent them down to reclaim them from those bestial Lifes, and to instruct them how to live happily and safely by observing such Laws, Customs, and Orders, as their Father the *Sun* had commanded these his Children to teach them. The great Rule they first taught was, That every Man should live according to Reason, and consequently neither say or do any Thing to others, that they were not willing others should say or do to them, because it was against all common Reason, to make one Law for ourselves, and another for other People. And this was the great Principle of all their Morality.[18]

The Houyhnhnms sound very close to these Ancients of the Ancients, though Swift might merely have taken these qualities and applied them to a race—somewhat the same sort of thing Lucretius conjectured—that existed before our present civilization had begun. Gulliver's identification of horses as "degenerate Houyhnhnms" would indicate that Swift intended his Houyhnhnms to be different creatures with a history of their own.

The yahoos and the Houyhnhnms are not, of course, historical. Swift has transformed them as any great artist creates, whatever the material he may be given. But the suggestion that they both grew out of not only what was possible, but what might have existed at different times in the past, should persuade us to allow something more than allegorical integrity to each.

The cyclic view, then, allows us to say that in the fourth voyage Swift brings together three civilizations—the English, the yahoos, and the Houyhnhnms. All three may be considered "real." At least all three grow from a seed of truth, and this gives them as much reality as they need for Swift's purposes. But the point is not so much that the yahoos and Houyhnhnms exist, or did exist; the point is that these three civilizations, at different stages, are significantly comparable. The Houyhnhnms are not created as an unreal, impossible ideal toward which all men should strive. If they were, then this voyage could represent only the blackest sort of pessimism, and in an unhappy critical procedure, Swift's letter to Pope —"I hate mankind. . . ."—has often been applied directly to this

voyage. But in spite of what Swift the man might say, the author of *Gulliver's Travels* did not hate mankind. He hated their irrational, immoral actions and their selfish, immoral philosophy as well. Viewed in their proper perspective, the Houyhnhnms are a symbol of hope, not despair. But they do not represent a goal which Gulliver himself can achieve; his forced departure symbolizes this point. These creatures are from the past. They represent the *perfection of nature.* They have followed natural reason to its ultimate end. But their animal form indicates the gulf that exists between man and Houyhnhnm. They stand for what has been, not what is. Why Swift made this distinction we can conjecture. The life of the Houyhnhnm is no longer possible because between the Ancients of the Ancients and Swift's own time stands Christian revelation. The Houyhnhnms, relying entirely upon natural reason, had reached perfection. Most of their ideals remain valid, but not complete enough for a creature shaped in the image of God.

As Swift examines the three civilizations of the fourth voyage, we should note first that he includes a great deal about each culture, and second that his account is based upon the same assumptions which we saw him use in the third voyage.

The survey of the third voyage has already been called inclusive. In the fourth voyage Swift is inclusive in a different way. In the third voyage, Swift made his point in terms of knowledge and learning. Beneath was a moral assumption, but it remained an assumption. In the fourth voyage, Swift is dealing directly with the moral nature of his creatures. His description of the English and the yahoos is a reasonably complete moral survey. He deals with the ethic of the individual, the family, and the nation; he makes an analysis of the morality of their conduct as individuals. He explains their government, and of course gives a physical description. The survey of the Houyhnhnms is even more detailed. Friendship, benevolence, and civility mark their relations with one another. These qualities may be seen within the family too, and in addition Swift shows their education, the reasonable nature of their courtship, and their relation to their children. On the personal level their temperance, industry, exercise, and health—all growing out of their devotion to reason—are illustrated in detail. They have no letters, only tradition—a quality of the Ancients of the Ancients which Temple remarks upon. They excel, as all Moderns admitted the Ancients did, in poetry, eloquence, and architecture—all three of which were, like their other knowledge, useful. Their attitude

toward death might well be called the triumph of their rational view of life.

Swift's assumptions in the fourth voyage are those already familiar from the second and the third. The chief is that man should direct his actions for the greatest good. He accomplishes this by letting his reason direct his choice. Although it is true that the Houyhnhnms are directed by reason and yahoos by their passions, it is a limitation of Swift's intent to say that they stand for these qualities. The satisfaction of the passions is an end for the yahoos, but for the Houyhnhnms the exercise of the reason is a means by which they establish and preserve their ethic. The greatest good for the greatest number is the end.

The fourth voyage is a *tour de force* of history, though Swift has more of the style of a magician of Glubbdubdrib than a careful historian. The yahoos, Gulliver, and the Houyhnhnms are different civilizations at different stages of development brought together for an eternal instant. We may marvel at them. We may judge them. But they are also authentic records. They show that perfection has been attained and therefore is still attainable. In Gulliver himself aspiration toward perfection is a vital force. He feels repugnance for the yahoos and veneration for the Houyhnhnms. But we can see more clearly than Gulliver. These creatures are more than moral standards. The yahoos are a measure of his progress from the past and the Houyhnhnms seem to promise tacitly that his hope for the future can be fulfilled.

Seeing a cyclical view of history in the fourth voyage naturally prompts the question whether it or something like it exists earlier in *Gulliver's Travels*.

All of the first three voyages contain human beings very much like Swift's contemporaries and describe recognizable human institutions. They represent three inherent possibilities of Western culture. The first voyage describes the present, Swift's own England. Temple, the source of the cyclic theory, has a statement that may help place Lilliput or, as Temple intended, modern England:

> Let it come about how it will, if we are Dwarfs, we are still so, though we stand upon a Giant's Shoulders; and even so placed, yet we see less than he, if we are naturally shorter sighted, or if we do not look as much about us, or if we are dazzled with the Height, which often happens from Weakness either of Heart or Brain.[19]

122

The first voyage is the point of departure for both the second and the third.

The second voyage is a view into the future—or toward what might have been—in a world that acts with some rationality. It represents a possible goal for man. Indeed, Temple suggests such a place might actually exist:

> But tho' there are or have been sometimes Dwarfs and sometimes Giants in the World, yet it does not follow, that there must be such in every Age nor in every Country: This we can no more conclude, than that there never have been any, because there are none now, at least in the Compass of our present Knowledge or Inquiry. As I believe, there may have been Giants at some Time, and some Place or other in the World, or such a Stature, as may not have been equalled perhaps again, in several Thousands of Years, or in any other Parts; so there may be Giants in Wit and Knowledge, or so over-grown a Size, as not to be equalled again in many Successions of Ages, or any Compass of Place or Country.[20]

The second voyage is a departure for the third. It reveals Swift's attitude toward the Moderns in the emphasis it gives to useful knowledge and in the King's rejection of gunpowder—the latter an especially symbolic act since gunpowder and the loadstone were the two chief Modern discoveries which defenders of the Ancients regarded as important.

The third voyage is a vision of the world based upon the ideals of the Modern Philosopher. Though the second voyage presents man in a state of only limited perfectibility, the third shows that he has a prodigious capacity for degeneration. The fundamentally unethical, anarchic society of the third voyage is a warning to modern man.

Gulliver's Travels is an excursion into time as well as into the realms of the imagination. Even without the historical panorama of the fourth voyage, the first three show that Swift is concerned not only with man's evil and folly, but with the dire consequences of present actions upon the future of civilization. All three books deal with man in a rather empirical way. They show his nature practically by presenting his institutions and his relationship with other men. These books are concerned primarily with the "dwarfs," as Temple called them. Briefly in the sixth chapter of the first book, the seventh of the second book, and the fourth of the third book, some of the positive assumptions underlying these voyages are revealed. These positive statements, especially those of the second voyage, are not always easy for modern readers to accept. It is sometimes difficult to realize that Swift and the modern reader may agree that certain actions are reprehensible without at all agreeing on what a proper action in the circumstances would be. Swift is not a modern intellectual, not even a modern. In order to justify both the ethic and the "positive" statements of *Gulliver's Travels,* we must accept the premise that all men should act in a way that brings happiness to all. Under such a premise, the first three books may be read as a coherent unit.

As it forms a part of a view of contemporary man's inherent possibilities, the third voyage functions with the first two. All three offer alternatives for human conduct. The third voyage is the vision of a false ideal, that of the Modern Philosopher. This voyage gives more than a mere view; it presents very nearly a totality. It is the world that would be created if the ideals of the Moderns were to prevail. Since their assumptions are basically immoral, their world is an anarchy rather than the paradise which they hopefully envision. The third part is thus vital to clarify Swift's moral assumptions.

But the third voyage plays a dual role in the structure of the work. It is a climax to the first three voyages, but it is also a counterpart to the fourth. Just as the third voyage is the ultimate expression of the Modern ideal, so the fourth contains the ultimate expression of the Ancient ideal. The third voyage shows the abuse of reason, though the depth of this abuse is not to be measured by silly experiments, but more profoundly by the misdirection of reason for ends not in the social good, immoral ends. The great virtue of the Houyhnhnms's reason is that it is directed toward ethical ends. The people of the third voyage represent the perfection of anarchy, the Houyhnhnms the perfection of nature. To the author of *Gulliver's Travels,* the difference between the Ancient and Modern view was a moral difference. Interpreted in this way, the third voyage is pivotal, providing a satiric climax for the first three books and a foreboding prophecy against which the fourth book stands.

In the last voyage Swift moves from a practical, limited view of man and his institutions, to a more general and philosophic view of man and his history. With its presentation of the savage and ideal states of time past, it provides the foil of history against which man of today and his false ideals may be judged. It does not, as history never does, present a solution. Gulliver embraces the Ancients as a solution only at the cost of separating himself from his own world. Swift nowhere asks that we follow Gulliver as an example, but he does hope to make the worlds of the second and third voyages more urgent and immediate by making us aware through Gulliver that we stand at a point in history and that we must choose. Just as the Ancients realized their potentialities, so we may realize ours. But progress is only one alternative; the specter of degeneration reminds us that we can easily fail.

Gulliver's Travels is a vision of past, present, and future. Those who see Swift as a satirist of his own times only, do him a great injustice. His view of society is dynamic. He upbraids his contemporaries for what they are, but he is also fundamentally concerned with what they might become. Without the frightening possibility of such a barren, wasted, futile future as we see in the third voyage, Lemuel Gulliver might never have left the shores of England.

Epilogue

Satire, like all literature, must ultimately be judged aesthetically, not in terms of its origin. Its conventions—in common with those of the love lyric, for example—are often highly personal and propagandistic, but in spite of appearance they are conventions, not fact. The objects of the satirist's art have been eternized, it is true, but like Stella and the Dark Lady, they live only in the poet's lines.

Satiric criticism has often made a distinction between a character like the Vicar of Wakefield, who appears in what might be called aesthetic satire, and characters like Achitophel and Atticus, who appear in personal satire and are often thought of as masks for real men. It is important to give a final answer to the question of whether there is, for the modern reader, a necessary distinction between these two kinds of characters.

A satirized character is an artistic construction. He exists as he can be seen in the values he holds or the actions he performs. In a good satire these values and actions are sufficient to motivate a character, though the author may profit from the preconceptions which his sympathetic contemporaries bring to the work. Dryden motivates Achitophel adequately within the work. Goldsmith does the same with the Vicar. Though Dryden's first readers may have seen only the Earl of Shaftesbury, the potential for universality has always been in the poem, and the modern reader's willingness to submerge Shaftesbury in the more significant Achitophel is a shift in emphasis rather than a reinterpretation.

There is no basic difference in satiric technique in the creation of the Vicar and Achitophel, only in the apparent source of the artist's materials and in his apparent purpose. There is a difference in effect as the known original of Achitophel introduces into the work values and emotions not overtly included by the author. In the course of time, extraneous values tend to be lost, and personal and aesthetic satire stand on the same level. It can never be said that one is "real" and the other "created." They vary only because the readers' knowledge of the authors' sources vary. Both are imaginative creations and have all the reality and only the reality of art.

The satirist, like any other artist, is basically a creator. His technique is ironic and he does attack, but only on the level of propa-

127

ganda could he be called merely negative. *Absalom and Achitophel* contains a complex system of values relating to religion, government, and family without which the attack would lack meaning. The foreboding fears of *Gulliver's Travels* touch the reader because he sees them against the moral system in which the author believes. Fundamentally the satirist is concerned with a contrast. In the great satires the contrast involves significant human values which appeal to men beyond the limits of one country or one time. As Richard Sympson said of his cousin Gulliver's travel book, "There is an air of truth apparent through the whole."

Notes

Notes

THE ANATOMY OF THE ART

1 Some of the good discussions are David Worcester, *The Art of Satire* (Cambridge, Mass., 1932); Ellen Leyburn, *Satiric Allegory: Mirror of Man* (New Haven, 1956); Ian Jack, *Augustan Satire: Intention and Idiom in English Poetry, 1660–1750* (Oxford, 1952); Alvin Kernan, *The Cankered Muse: Satire of the English Renaissance* (New Haven, 1959); James Sutherland, *English Satire* (Cambridge, 1958); Robert C. Elliott, *The Power of Satire: Magic, Ritual, Art* (Princeton, 1960); Richmond P. Bond, *English Burlesque Poetry, 1700–1750* (Cambridge, Mass., 1932); Mary Claire Randolph, "The Structural Design of the Formal Verse Satire," *Philological Quarterly*, XXI (1942), 368–84; and especially Maynard Mack, "The Muse of Satire," *Yale Review*, XLI (1951), 80–92. The most thoroughgoing attempt to analyze irony and satire and to give them a place in a theory of criticism is Northrop Frye, *Anatomy of Criticism* (Princeton, 1957).

2 Two good discussions of the persona occur in Mack, *op. cit.*, and in William B. Ewald, Jr., *The Masks of Jonathan Swift* (Oxford, 1954).

3 The satirist's purpose is discussed by Louis I. Bredvold, "A Note in Defence of Satire," *E L H*, VII (1940), 253–64.

4 Elder Olson, "Rhetoric and the Appreciation of Pope," *Modern Philology*, XXXVII (1939), 13–35.

5 *Modern Language Notes*, XLVIII (1933), 1–11.

THE RAPE OF THE LOCKE and THE RAPE OF THE LOCK

1 "At any rate, the poem was written; its beauties and its reputation have little connection with the original circumstances." Bond, pp. 64–65.

2 The additions made by Pope are listed in *The Twickenham Edition of the Poems of Alexander Pope: The Rape of the Lock and Other Poems*, ed. Geoffrey Tillotson (London, 1940), II, 123. Quotations follow this edition.

3 Religious implications are discussed by Austin Warren, "The Mask of Pope," *Sewanee Review*, LIV (1946), 19–33.

4 Cleanth Brooks, "The Case of Miss Arabella Fermor," *The Well Wrought Urn: Studies in the Structure of Poetry* (New York, c1947), pp. 80–104. Brooks' reading is a good deal more satisfactory than that of Hugo Reichard, "The Love Affair in Pope's 'Rape of the Lock'," *Publications of the Modern Language Association*, LXIX (1954), 887–902. Reichard calls the Baron an uninhibited philanderer, Belinda an invincible flirt and holds that her falling in love does not affect her status or her further adventures.

5 By dividing his action into five cantos, Pope heightens the apparent epic parody. James Jackson, "The *Rape of the Lock* as a Five-Act Epic," *Publications of the Modern Language Association*, LXV (1950), 1283–87. Additional epic parody is not of great moment; the new structure, as the discussion shows, is significant.

ABSALOM AND ACHITOPHEL

1 The historical and cultural dimension of the poem has been explored significantly in different ways by Richard F. Jones, "The Originality of *Absalom and Achitophel*," *Modern Language Notes*, XLVI (1931), 211–18; E. S. de Beer, "Absalom and Achitophel: Literary and Historical Notes," *Review of English Studies*, XVII (1941), 298–309; Ruth Wallerstein, "To Madness Near Allied: Shaftesbury and His Place in the Design and Thought of *Absalom and Achitophel*," *Huntington Library Quarterly*, VI (1943), 445–71; and Godfrey Davies, "The Conclusion of Dryden's *Absalom and Achitophel*," *Huntington Library Quarterly*, X (1946), 69–82. The most detailed attempt to place the poem politically is Bernard Schilling, *Dryden and the Conservative Myth: A Reading of "Absalom and Achitophel"* (New Haven, 1961).
2 References to the poem follow *The Poems of John Dryden*, ed. James Kinsley (Oxford, 1958), I.
3 The parallel has been discussed by Morris Friedman, "Dryden's Miniature Epic," *Journal of English and Germanic Philology*, LVII (1958), 211–19 and A. B. Chambers, "Absalom and Achitophel: Christ and Satan," *Modern Language Notes*, LXXIV (1959), 592–96.

HUDIBRAS *and The Nature of Man*

1 Leyburn, *op. cit.*
2 *ELH*, XVIII (1951), 7–31.
3 Dan Gibson, Jr., "Samuel Butler," *Seventeenth Century Studies*, ed. Robert Shafer (Princeton, 1933), 279–335.
4 "Butler," *Lives of the English Poets by Samuel Johnson, Lld.*, ed. George Birkbeck Hill (Oxford, 1905), I, 211.
5 Quotations are from Samuel Butler, *Hudibras*, ed. A. R. Waller (Cambridge, 1905). The lines of the text are not numbered. Citations show the part, canto, and page number.
6 Quintana, "Samuel Butler," p. 27.
7 Leyburn, p. 47.

ARBUTHNOT'S *Simple Plan*

1 Francis B. Thornton, *Alexander Pope: Catholic Poet* (New York, 1952), p. 228.
2 Rebecca Price Parkin, *The Poetic Workmanship of Alexander Pope* (Minneapolis, 1955), pp. 18f. Modern criticism of Pope owes

a debt to Maynard Mack, whose assumptions and approach are illustrated in "On Reading Pope," *College English,* VII (1946), 263–73.

3 Robert W. Rogers, *The Major Satires of Alexander Pope* (Urbana, 1955), pp. 86ff. The development of the poem is also discussed by Elder Olson, "Rhetoric and the Appreciation of Pope," *Modern Philology,* XXXVII (1939), 13–35 and by Elias F. Mengel, Jr., "Patterns of Imagery in Pope's *Arbuthnot,*" *Publications of the Modern Language Association,* LXIX (1954), 189–97.

4 Rogers, "Appendix D," p. 133.

5 References are to *The Twickenham Edition of the Poems of Alexander Pope: Imitations of Horace with an Epistle to Dr Arbuthnot and the Epilogue to the Satires,* ed. John Butt (London, 1939), IV.

6 A detailed examination of the actual relationship of the two men has been made by Norman Ault, "Pope and Addison," *Review of English Studies,* XVII (1941), 428–51. Susanne K. Langer in "Poetic Creation," *Problems of Art* (New York, 1957), discusses the problem of "facts" in poetry.

7 Ault shows that he did not. See pp. 443–51.

THE VICAR OF WAKEFIELD *and The Kindly Satirist*

1 W. F. Gallaway, Jr., "The Sentimentalism of Goldsmith," *Publications of the Modern Language Association,* XLVIII (1933), 1167–81.

2 Frederick W. Hilles' introduction to the Modern Library edition of *The Vicar of Wakefield* distinguishes between the mood and tone of the early and later parts of the book. A thematic motif is discussed by Curtis Dahl, "Patterns of Disguise in *The Vicar of Wakefield,*" *E L H,* XXV (1958), 90–104.

3 Quotations follow the Modern Library edition of *The Vicar of Wakefield and Other Writings,* ed. Frederick W. Hilles (New York, c1955).

The Plot of RASSELAS

1 Gwin J. Kolb offered the first detailed and comprehensive argument for structural unity in *Rasselas* in "The Structure of *Rasselas,*" *Publications of the Modern Language Association,* LXVI (1951), 698–717. Later Alvin Whitley, seeing the same sort of unity, argued further that "*Rasselas* was a satire on the illusioned view of life" and Rasselas himself an illusioned visionary. "The Comedy of *Rasselas,*" *E L H,* XXIII (1956), 48–70.

2 Joseph Wood Krutch, *Samuel Johnson* (New York, c1944), p. 182.

3 Whitley, *op.cit.,* argues that there is.

4 *Rasselas,* ed. George Birkbeck Hill (Oxford, 1958), p. 44.

5 *Ibid.*, p. 52.
6 *Ibid.*, p. 70.
7 *Ibid.*, p. 157.
8 Hawkins' characterization of *Rasselas* as "general satire" is well known. *The Life of Samuel Johnson, LL.D., by Sir John Hawkins, Knt.*, Edited, Abridged, and with an Introduction by Bertram H. Davis (New York, 1961), p. 156, is a convenient location.
9 *Rasselas*, pp. 91f.
10 *Ibid.*, p. 67.
11 *Ibid.*, p. 157.

GULLIVER'S THIRD VOYAGE

1 Reprinted in Marjorie Nicholson, *Science and Imagination* (Ithaca, 1956).
2 John Middleton Murry, *Jonathan Swift: A Critical Biography* (London, 1954), p. 331.
3 Ricardo Quintana, *Swift: An Introduction* (London, 1955), p. 161.
4 Kathleen Williams, *Jonathan Swift and the Age of Compromise* (Lawrence, Kans., 1959), pp. 175ff.
5 John Sutherland, "A Reconsideration of Gulliver's Third Voyage," *Studies in Philology*, LIV (1957), 45–52.
6 William Wotton, *Reflections upon Ancient and Modern Learning*, 3d edition, corrected (London, 1705).
7 Quotations from Temple's essays follow *The Works of Sir William Temple, Bart.* (London, 1740), 2 vols.
8 Temple, I, 199.
9 Clara Marburgh, *Sir William Temple: A Seventeenth Century "Libertin"* (New Haven, 1932), p. 42.
10 *Gulliver's Travels, 1726, With an Introduction by Harold Williams*, The Prose Works of Jonathan Swift, ed. Herbert Davis (Oxford, 1941), XI, 119f.
11 John F. Ross, "The Final Comedy of Lemuel Gulliver," *University of California Publications in English*, VIII (1941), 175–96.
12 Wotton, p. viii.
13 *Gulliver's Travels*, pp. 255f.
14 Temple, I, 153.
15 *Ibid.*, I, 156.
16 *Ibid.*, I, 158.
17 *Ibid.*, I, 200.
18 *Ibid.*, I, 207.
19 *Ibid.*, I, 159.
20 *Ibid.*